DER

ALLOTMENT &

Garden Guide

Twigs Way

SABRESTORM

Designed and typeset by Philip Clucas MSIAD

British Library Cataloguing in Publication Data

A catalogue record for this book is available from the British Library

Published by
Sabrestorm Publishing,
90 Lennard Road,
Dunton Green,
Sevenoaks, Kent TN13 2UX

Website: www.sabrestorm.com

Email: books@sabrestorm.com

ISBN 978-0-9552723-5-6

Contents

This Dig for Victory poster encourages the growing of vegetables for the sake of the children whose expectant faces can be seen. *(HMSO)*

Introduction

Produced by the Ministry of Agriculture, the *Allotment & Garden Guides* were issued monthly throughout 1945. Aimed at the amateur gardener they were to be the final rallying call in the wartime campaign to Dig for Victory. Although they did not carry the actual 'Dig for Victory' slogan, the Guides included the famous foot and spade logo that had become universally recognised since its introduction five years earlier. In fact the government had been experimenting with new slogans in an attempt to keep up enthusiasm, including 'Dig for Plenty' and 'Dig for Peace', but none had quite that 'victory' ring, and in an effort to make the Guides appear as similar as possible to the 'normal' gardening periodicals, headline slogans were quietly dropped.

Concentrating exclusively on the productive garden, the Guides were designed to take the novice or amateur gardener through the basic tasks of each month. Published in the last year of war, and extending into the post-war austerity period, the Guides combine patriotic fervour with practical horticulture.

Many of the subjects tackled are as relevant now as they were then: How to Make a Compost Heap, When to Sow Marrow Seed, Which Seeds are Easiest to Save, are all still popular topics in the modern gardening media. However other subjects covered are redolent of wartime difficulties: continuing seed shortages due to enemy

Above: *A wartime photograph of a young boy in the garden.*
Children were encouraged to do their bit in the wartime garden, even
if it was just related to the hunting and destroying of garden pests.

occupation in Europe, regulations on flower growing, and the very real prospect of running out of food next winter.

Some of the recommended tasks would now be illegal (spray plants liberally with nicotine), while others that were illegal would now be recommended (feeding birds with waste food). Many people still work allotment or vegetable plots that were first established during the war years, 'inheriting' them from a generation that used these Guides as their gardening bibles. To read the Guides now is to experience a sense both of the urgency of work in the wartime garden, and the timelessness of the processes of gardening.

Background

On the 3rd October 1939, Sir Reginald Dorman-Smith, Minister for Agriculture, announced what was to become one of the most successful and memorable government campaigns ever. Initiated exactly a month after Britain entered the Second World War, the campaign to Grow More Food (eventually called the Dig for Victory campaign) captured the spirits, and the stomachs, of all those who did their bit on the Home Front. In 1938 Britain had imported some 55 million tons of food, food that for the next six years would have to be grown at home. On the frontline of this campaign were the nation's vegetable gardens and allotments.

With over 500,000 new allotments being made available by the government almost immediately, and a further 500,000 in September 1940, the allotment army alone was to enlist over 3 million by the end of the war. By 1945 it was estimated that half of all working class households cultivated an allotment or tended a plot within their own garden and some district councils claimed to provide a plot for every other household. Private lawns, public parks, town squares and even country house pleasure grounds were dug up everywhere and made to 'do their bit' for the war effort. Emergency powers permitted the requisitioning of land of all types to help feed the nation. Beans became munitions, carrots replaced sweets and onions briefly became worth their weight in gold.

Along with so many new garden plots came so many novice gardeners and, having persuaded them into the garden, the government was bound to provide them with instruction on what to do when they got there. For the first few months of the war this instruction took the form of the Growmore Food Bulletins. The first bulletin, in fact more a substantial booklet than a brief bulletin, was issued in October

1939. Entitled 'Food from the Garden' this guide to all things essential for growing your own had in fact been in preparation for several months in the run-up to war. This did not prevent some teething problems. Professional gardeners pounced on ill-advised spacing and varieties unsuited to northern climes but, as the government pointed out, at least there was some guidance available for everyone.

After only one year and four bulletins, the Growmore Food campaign was in need of a re-launch. The bulletins had proved to be rather too long and too detailed for the novice gardener, and topics such as 'Pests and Diseases' were not as popular as it might have been hoped. People were also unwilling to pay the 4d cost.

October 1940 saw the official launch of the new Dig for Victory campaign, with the famous logo of a (left) foot on a spade. It was modelled by a Mr W.H. McKie of Acton (London). A new series of full-page advertisements accompanied the re-launch, encouraging new gardeners to do their bit for the nation's larder, a larder which was notably running short. Onions had become one of the first casualties of the war followed by a shortage of potatoes, a shortage which may have done more to encourage the 'grow your own' mentality than any government propaganda.

A vital element of the re-launched campaign was the production of a new range of simpler, shorter leaflets. These new leaflets were free and were to be distributed in their millions, continuing to be available long after the end of the war. Between 1940 and 1944 the government issued twenty-six leaflets on a wide range of topics, from Potato Blight

Right: *An important aspect of the Dig for Victory campaign was the need to provide food all year round, not just summer salads. (HMSO)*

Your own vegetables all the year round ...

PRINTED FOR H.M. STATIONERY OFFICE
BY W. R. ROYLE & SON, LTD.   51-2095

if you

DIG FOR VICTORY NOW

to Window Box Gardening. With the aid of these leaflets it was meant to be possible for even the most inexperienced gardener to produce food for themselves and their family.

Radio programmes such as '*In Your Garden*', or the BBC's '*Radio Allotment*' gave further advice, while books and magazines endlessly repeated the basic mantras of plan, plant and protect from pests. However, by the winter of 1944 even the specialist gardening periodicals were running out of steam and it was left to the government once again to pick up the baton with its new series of *Allotment & Garden Guides*.

The Aim of the Guides

Issued from January 1945 onwards, the *Allotment & Garden Guides* came out monthly. Their purpose, as outlined in the very first issue, was: *To remind you of the things that ought to have been done, but may not have been possible because of the weather or for some other reason; to deal with garden operations for that month; and to look ahead a month or two and remind you of what you need to do in readiness.'* Basically Panic, Plant and Plan!

Being monthly they could not take into account short-term weather fluctuations and so the writers of the Guides recommended that people also took a weekly gardening journal or looked at the gardening feature in their newspaper. It may seem odd that with more topical information available elsewhere, the government decided to issue these monthly 'newsletters', but they wanted to ensure that as many people as possible appreciated the urgent need to continue gardening, and most importantly continued to plant and produce the crops that would see the country through not just the summer months, but also the long harsh winters.

In the very first weeks of the war the government had circulated its ideal cropping plan for an allotment-sized plot, a cropping plan designed specifically to avoid shortages or gluts at different times of year. This tried to steer people away from over-enthusiastic planting of lettuces and strawberries by focusing on winter and spring greens, such as kale and spring cabbage. Talking about planning the next year's campaign on the plot, the February Guide noted that *'if your wife, or whoever runs the kitchen department, complains that there is little or nothing in the garden and that shop prices are high, it would pay you to plan so that you grow your own winter vegetables – especially greens'*.

Although almost all of the information in the gardening press and national newspapers adhered closely to the government's recommendations during the war years, the military successes of the summer of 1944 had seen the return of articles dwelling on the delights of the flower bed and laying of lawns. By providing free information in the form of what appeared to be a 'normal' gardening periodical, the government hoped to keep people focused on vegetables and away from flowers. Although by 1945 allotment holders were technically permitted to use a small area of their plots for growing flowers, 'a happy fringe' was the phrase used in one newspaper, the *Allotment & Garden Guides* never included instruction on flower growing. The March 1945 edition notes the new 'relaxed' rules on flower planting, but hastily moves on to recommendations for 'wholesome radishes' and autumn-sown onions. Brassicas, beans, potatoes, leeks, cabbages and Brussels sprouts were the lot of the Garden Guides. Despite being published right through 1945, the *Allotment & Garden Guides* do not mention either VE Day or VJ Day. The luxuries of peace had no place in the productive garden and May, June, July, August and September passed by with no let-up of effort. Even the final guide made no mention of the peaceful years on the horizon, instead expressing the hope that wartime gardeners would find themselves tightly bound to the '*most enduring hobby of all*'.

What To Grow?

The *Allotment & Garden Guides* adhered almost exclusively to the crops recommended in the Ministry of Agriculture's Dig for Victory Leaflet No. 1. However, they acknowledged that there might be some alterations needed according to location (tomatoes did not do well in the north of the country!) and soil conditions. They even generously permitted some variation according to the likes and dislikes of the family. The March Guide suggested that '*You can still get the Ministry's cropping plan, not to follow it blindly, but to use it as a guide that you can adapt to meet your family's likes and dislikes and modify in the light of your knowledge of the kinds of vegetables that can be grown satisfactorily in your neighbourhood'*.

Following the cropping plan in the Dig for Victory Leaflet No. 1 would have provided you with onions, shallots, leeks, lettuce, cabbages, savoys, spinach (summer and winter,) 'Brussels', sprouting

RUTH MORGAN'S WARTIME COOKERY

KITCHEN GARDEN
pickles

The more pickles, chutneys and preserves
you can make now, the simpler it will be to
plan meals through the winter months ahead

Above: *Newspapers and magazines produced many recipes, ideas and articles on how home-grown summer fruit and vegetables could be preserved for the winter months.*

broccoli, kale, carrots, beet[root], parsnips, turnips or swedes, broad beans, runner beans, peas and of course potatoes. Marrows could be grown on the compost heap and radishes as an inter-crop. Marrows were cut large and mature while the closely related courgette was regarded as a foreigner, almost as unknown as the eggplant or okra. More adventurous gardeners might grow Jerusalem artichokes, kohl rabi, herbs (tackled rather oddly in the December Garden Guide) and celeriac. Celery was widely regarded as a difficult and time-consuming crop, as were cauliflowers. Haricot beans, encouraged by the government as being a good protein source, were not widely popular.

Asparagus was officially discouraged as being a 'luxury' crop, providing little food in return for much attention, and hogging precious space year round. Cucumbers were also discouraged as providing little nutrition in return for much care.

Few people could obtain good crops without some form of heating or glass. Tomatoes on the other hand were encouraged as being nutritious, popular and tasty. Regarded as essential in salads, they were also used in some cooked foods, although the widespread use of pasta and tomato sauces lay in the distant future in the 1940s, and sun-dried tomatoes were unheard of. Prior to the war tomatoes had been imported from Europe and the Channel Islands. With the occupation of the Channel Islands in June 1940 home-grown tomatoes were the order of the day. Dig for Victory Leaflet No. 8 instructed the populace on tomato growing and proved to be one of the most popular of the Victory leaflets, despite the difficulties of raising tomatoes in the poor summers that dogged many of the war years. The May Guide reflected ruefully on the lack of sun in the previous year (1944) and warned tomato growers not to put plants out until at least 20th May, and further north not until mid-June, in an attempt to escape the late frosts.

After tomatoes, potatoes were the next favourite crop of many gardeners and cooks. A staple of the British diet, the Ministry of Agriculture recommended that gardeners should plant nine rows of potatoes, comprising three rows of 'earlies' and six rows of main crop. Many gardeners had to be restrained from planting even more rows of this invaluable vegetable, which grew with little difficulty and stored easily. In 1940 and 1941 there had been a shortage of potatoes as many farmers had turned to wheat crops, and imported supplies had simultaneously ground to a halt. The Ministry of Agriculture, which had until that point insisted that potatoes should be a low priority for amateur gardeners, had taken out advertisements asking householders to grow more potatoes, although not at the expense of winter greens.

As wheat supplies in turn faltered, the 'Potato Pete' campaign emphasised the importance of the humble potato as an essential source of energy. But by then the government was confident that farmers and market gardeners would be able to supply the shops, and householders were told once more to restrict themselves to the recommended nine rows. Given these fluctuations, it may have come as a surprise to many gardeners to read in the March Garden Guide that *'Throughout the war the Ministry has been consistent in its advice that the household grower should not overdo potatoes (as many are apt to).'*

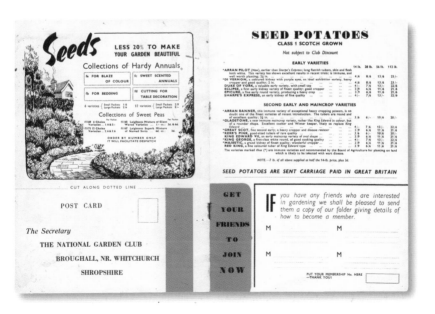

Above: *Potatoes were a favourite with many gardeners and the advice was to purchase seed potatoes in plenty of time and only from trusted suppliers.*

MINISTRY of AGRICULTURE

WAR TIME CAMPAIGN
GROW MORE FOOD

Certificate of Merit

Awarded to

John Rawlinson

who cultivated a plot of land to the
best advantage and so made a valuable
contribution towards the Nation's effort
to grow more food in time of war

James Berakes

MAYOR OF BOLTON

R. S. Hudson

MINISTER OF AGRICULTURE AND FISHERIES

1943

OMNIA VINCIT LABOR

Above: *Certificates of Merit were awarded to allotment
holders whose plots were judged to be efficiently producing
crops throughout the year.*

Obtaining seed potato was a concern for home growers and many either used some of last year's potatoes, or divided the nurseryman's seed potato into halves or even quarters. Some even tried to use potato peel as a 'seed' source. Unsurprisingly yields amongst home growers were often far below the levels expected from the farmer or market gardener, especially where manure or fertiliser was in short supply. The January and February Guides both warned against using seed potato that did not come from a regulated supplier, and gardeners were constantly reminded to order in good time to allow supplies to reach them in the face of transport difficulties.

Generally speaking the Guides did not recommend specific varieties of vegetables and fruits. There were two main reasons for this. Firstly the Guides were trying to cater for all types of soil and conditions from south to north, east to west. Secondly, and perhaps more importantly, the war years had seen extreme fluctuations in the availability of different varieties of vegetable seeds. Early versions of the Dig for Victory leaflets which had recommended specific varieties had led to a 'rush' on these, which meant that supplies ran out and the leaflets had to be reprinted with different varieties. The situation fluctuated throughout the war, getting marginally better as home-grown supplies increased. Even so the January Guide reminded gardeners that: *'Before the war many of our seeds came from countries that were until recently under enemy control, and while we can still get most kinds, certain varieties – perhaps your favourites – may be short'*. Novice gardeners were often recommended to leave the choice in the hands of their local seedsman. Potatoes were an exception as the supply of seed potatoes was regulated, but even then the Guide carefully stated that *'here are some selected varieties for your guidance'*. Saving your own vegetable seeds was also popular, and the

July Guide gave instruction on how to do this, a worthwhile task in the years before the F1 hybrid, and something that the government encouraged for certain types of vegetables.

Manure

Essential to any good garden, manure was on everyone's mind in wartime and was one of the most popular topics for the Guides. Organic manure was in extremely short supply during the war, in part due to the huge increase in gardeners, but also due to prioritising the needs of farmers and market gardeners. Farmyard manures (horse, pig, etc) were almost impossible for the ordinary gardener to obtain, although as more people joined the 'backyarder' movement and raised their own poultry, chicken manure became easier to obtain. The 'secret pig' (many were kept unofficially) was also a precious source of manure. Organic materials that were available, at least in the first years of the war, included hoof and horn meal, dried blood, meat and bone meal, shoddy (waste from textile processing) and soot. Soot was easy to obtain as most houses still had coal fires in the 1940s, but had to be 'weathered' before it could be used. The old favourite of guano (the accumulated phosphate-rich droppings of birds, seals and bats) was extremely difficult to get as it had to be brought in by ship.

As the war dragged on, all types of organic manure became difficult to obtain. In response the government tried to encourage two substitutes: home-made compost and artificial fertilisers. Home-made compost could be created by anyone with space for a small compost heap and a supply of vegetable waste. Compost heaps, now a common sight in allotments, were almost unknown before the war except in large country house gardens, and the Ministry of Agriculture had quickly brought out a special Dig for Victory Leaflet (Leaflet No. 7) on How to

Above: *This official publicity photograph of a well-dressed woman applying fertiliser to an allotment in Kensington Gardens shows how every opportunity was taken to utilise space for food production. (HMSO)*

Make a Compost Heap. Although compost could help keep up the organic and 'humic' content of the soil, especially useful on poor soils and soils with high clay content, home-made compost under wartime conditions rarely provided the right ratio of essential foods for the plants to grow well. Artificial fertilisers were to be the answer to this problem.

Although artificial fertilisers had met with some distrust amongst amateur gardeners, the shortage of organic manures led to a rush on these 'artificials'. Before the outbreak of war, Britain had imported agricultural chemical fertilisers from the continent, most notably potash from mines in Germany and France. These were now almost impossible to obtain. Phosphate present in slag from ironworks, which had also been readily available, was now diverted for military use causing another shortage. To add to these difficulties, novice gardeners were also prone to using too much or too little of the essential trio of nitrogen, phosphate and potash and thus causing an imbalance in the soil. To try and counter these two problems, in 1942 the government introduced its own National Growmore fertiliser. The fertiliser contained a balance of 7% of each of the main plant foods of potash, phosphate and nitrogen. Each allotment holder was recommended to apply 42lb of National Growmore to his 10-rod [300-square yards] plot: 30lb as general dressing in advance of sowing or planting, and the final 12lb as an 'extra' dressing for winter crops and the ever-hungry potatoes. After the war, research indicated that this was actually a very low rate of application and most plots would have benefited from more.

In addition to fertilisers and manures (when they could get them), gardeners were advised to add a variety of other chemicals to their soil. Foremost amongst these was lime. The *Allotment & Garden Guides* first drew the attention of their readers to the importance of adding lime in January, and repeated the reminders in February and then again in October, when details of different types of lime were discussed. One of the reason for this extended discussion was the shortage of lime. Hydrated lime was the most popular type amongst gardeners, but what little there was available had been allocated to farmers and also, in the immediate post-war period, to builders. The October Guide tried to persuade gardeners to use carbonate lime from chalk or limestone instead. Allotment and Gardening Societies could order lime in bulk at half price from a special department of the Ministry of Agriculture under the Government's Land Fertility Scheme.

Above: *Specialist magazines offered advice to new gardeners although many relied on gardening columns in their regular newspapers. The 'Dig to Eat' slogan was not a government preferred slogan, being considered too defeatist.*

Crop Rotation

At the outset of the Dig for Victory campaign, crop rotation over several years had been recommended only cautiously. Although a standard technique to ensure better quality crops, the government was wary of admitting to the many new Victory gardeners that the war might last for three years or more. By 1945 crop rotation was essential if allotments and vegetable plots hastily laid out on often poor soils were to continue producing decent yields. Rotation also allowed gardeners to restrict their precious manure and fertiliser to areas that were earmarked for especially 'hungry' crops.

Treasured farmyard manure was kept for the peas, beans, leeks and onions section. This was then followed by cabbages and other winter greens in the next year. Benefiting from the previous year's manure, and the nitrogen fixed by the peas and beans, this would receive just a light dressing of National Growmore Fertiliser. In the third year of the rotation this area would be planted with potatoes and other roots. Over-fertilising the root crop led to forked carrots and parsnips and so the remaining Growmore fertiliser and any 'spare' manure could be used in the potato trenches.

Trenching was also more commonly used for runner beans and peas than it is now, and where these followed root crops, the soil would have been thoroughly dug over for two years running before being used for the brassicas, which preferred firm soil. This long-term planning was something that many novice gardeners found difficult, preferring to put rows in as space became available and hoping that the war would soon be over! However the *Allotment & Garden Guides* stressed that crop rotation *'is the only sound basis for vegetable growing'*.

Pests and Wildlife

Nearly every month's edition of the *Allotment & Garden Guide* saw admonitions to spray sulphur, dust with Derris or crush caterpillars. Pests were seen as enemies not only of the garden but of the nation as a whole. The popular press ran campaigns featuring rats with Hitler moustaches and millipedes with swastika flags (also featured in the April edition of the Guide, *right*), while topical slogans such as 'Hold pests at the Maginot Line' became popular. The November Guide looked back on a year that had seen *'the biggest invasion from the*

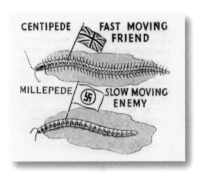

Continent since 1940': fortunately an invasion of 'cabbage white' butterflies. Dusting against the dreaded cabbage white should have commenced in March according to the Guides, and further warnings were issued in April (with a picture for identification), and again in July, with an alarming cartoon of a 6ft tall caterpillar! As well as the cabbage white caterpillar, pests and diseases of all kinds beset the gardener.

Blackfly, whitefly, greenfly, flea beetle, carrot fly, cabbage root fly, millipedes, wireworm, leather jackets, slugs, snails, mildew, fruit scab and 'club root' disease all needed elimination by the favourite methods of the day: spraying with poisonous chemicals. The notion of organic

Above: *Even if you did not have an allotment or garden of your own, you were still encouraged to do your bit helping out with food production.*

or wildlife-friendly gardening was almost unknown in the 1940s, and was certainly not promoted by the government. Instead gardeners were encouraged to mix up their own killer sprays. Derris, nicotine, metaldehyde ('meta') and naphthalene were all common, often as powders to be made up into dry or wet sprays. Of these, nicotine was recognised as dangerous if handled or mixed incautiously, while 'meta' occasionally poisoned small animals or pets by being mixed in bread or bran which incautious animals gobbled up before the slugs could get to it. Fruit trees and bushes did not escape the sprays, and the very first guide recommended spending any sunny winter days spraying fruit trees and currants with a tar-oil spray. March saw the same trees and currants being sprayed with lime sulphur to ward off mildew, scab and 'big bud'. Although DDT (now banned) was in use by the armed forces by 1945, it was not in common use in amateur horticulture or agriculture until the 1950s.

Although at times it seemed as if anything that could crawl or fly was the avowed enemy of the 1940s' gardener, there were exceptions. In the December issue of the Guide there was a short piece on how to feed and help maintain the 'useful insect-eating birds' of gardens and suburbs. These included the robin, the wren, the hedge sparrow and the various species of tits. Bird tables laden with titbits of food and fat may seem obvious to us, but in wartime it was actually illegal to 'waste' human food, and 'waste' included feeding it to animals (even backyard hens and rabbits). Instead the Guide suggested that the birds would enjoy fish skin and bones, crumbs, and cheese rind or '*bits of fat from the dog's meat man*'. It was unlikely that the dog's meat man was doing much of a brisk trade in wartime anyway as the government had discouraged people from pet owning, fearing that animals might run wild if abandoned when families were evacuated.

Nest-boxes for birds was the other suggestion made to help keep numbers up (and insects down). Rather wonderfully the Ministry of Agriculture had created a special leaflet on building wartime nest-boxes (Advisory Leaflet No. 212), and readers of the Guide were recommended to send for this. Bird identification had been the subject of an article in the May edition, dividing the feathered friends from the feathered enemies. House sparrows, pigeons and jays were all seen as possible enemies, stealing peas and uprooting seedlings. It was the tits, the great insect collectors, and the thrushes, enemies of snails and slugs, that were regarded as the real champions.

Other wildlife to escape the censure of the Ministry of Agriculture was the humble centipede, patriotically illustrated with a Union Jack in the April Guide and the aphid-eating ladybird. Although, only extraordinarily tough lady-birds would have survived the onslaught of chemicals.

Left and **opposite page:** *Women were rarely seen on the allotment before the war. They were more often shown in the kitchen preparing the food. As the war progressed and manpower was in even shorter supply, many ended up doing both jobs.*

Women in the Garden

Rarely seen on vegetable plots or allotment sites before the war, women were now the focus of a sustained government campaign to get them out of the home and into the garden. Photographs of women digging plots in Kensington Gardens *(see page 23)*, posing with fork in hand on numerous bombsite gardens, or almost hidden behind piles of freshly picked produce,

had been used to spread the word that vegetables were not just for men! In wartime gardening magazines, letters pages included enquiries sent by women concerning everything from mealy bug to how to grow and process sugar beet! After 1942, by which time manpower was in even shorter supply, 'Home Front' gardening pages filled with news of successful women allotment holders single-handedly raising families, holding down jobs and working several plots. Some women even gained the much vaunted Certificate of Merit for their work on their plots, while many more just got down to the job in hand of raising food to feed the family.

The government set itself a target of attracting over 10,000 women onto their own allotment plots, although it realised that many more already made important contributions to the war effort by cultivating plots left vacant as husbands and brothers had gone off to fight. The producers of the *Allotment & Garden Guides* do not seem to have paid any attention to this vision of equality on the vegetable plot, and only included two images of women in the whole year of Guides. In June a well-dressed and immaculately groomed lady picked a rose to illustrate '*the month of leaves and roses*', while in April a pair of young girls represented '*April's girlish laughter and tears*': hardly the image to get women out onto the plot or impress members of the Women's Land Army! Women did get one other look-in in the Garden Guides – back in the kitchen. In December the Guide recommended copies of the Ministry of Agriculture's old bulletins 'Preserves from the Garden' (4d) and 'Domestic Preservation of Fruit and Vegetables' (1s 6d) as suitable Christmas presents for '*the lady of the family*'. Those taking up the suggestion (in particular the cheaper 3d bulletin) may have found they had a less than happy Christmas!

Lighter Moments

With its emphasis on the very real battle against starvation, there was little space in the Guides for light-hearted banter. However, the authors obviously felt that there should be some lightening of the tone and so from February onwards most of the guides opened with a short poem or couplets appropriate to the month in question. Many of these were weather-related: such as February's reminder that '*February Fill Dyke*' and that gardeners might expect either rain or snow to hinder their operations that month, or April's '*Laugh thy girlish laughter; Then, the moment after, Weep thy girlish tears*' (a rather fanciful way of alluding to 'April showers'). Others were of a more poetic nature: June was saluted as '*The month of leaves and roses, When pleasant sights salute the eyes, And pleasant scents the noses*' and September held a

Right: *The December Guide suggested 'Preserves from the Garden' as a practical gift for the lady of the family.*

PRESERVES FROM THE GARDEN

SUGAR

"GROWMORE" BULLETIN No. 3
OF THE MINISTRY OF AGRICULTURE
AND FISHERIES PUBLISHED BY
HIS MAJESTY'S STATIONERY OFFICE

PRICE 4d. NET

Estancia by **joyce** *(CALIFORNIA)*

Nowadays, there are marrows instead of fairies at the bottom of the garden, and you are far more concerned with the state of the spinach than with the size of the chrysanthemum blooms . . . The lady of shallots will find that **joyce** *has matched such a practical outlook with this Estancia model. —It boasts no frills but—its comfort has very deep roots—and as for hard wear, it certainly knows how many beans make five . . . .*

JOYCE (CALIFORNIA) LIMITED, 17-18 OLD BOND STREET, LONDON, W.1 (WHOLESALE ONLY)

Above: *Advertisements were often linked to the Dig for Victory campaign and stressed how the products could benefit the wartime gardener.*

promise of *'exceeding joy hereafter'*. Most of the verses were traditional sayings or well-known couplets or verses, but November saw a verse by the early 19th-century writer Thomas Hood and December readers were treated to an excerpt from Keats.

The first peacetime Christmas also saw a distinct relaxation of tone in the December 1945 Garden Guide (the last of the series). A range of garden-related Christmas presents were suggested including tools and seeds, books and bulbs. A pinch of onion seed from a variety hard to get, or a clump of chives might look unexciting in December, but would prove useful in the coming summer. Less popular with the recipient might have been a selection of 'left-over' Growmore Food Bulletins on subjects such as 'Pests and Diseases'. A subscription to a gardening magazine might have been especially useful given that no more garden Guides were issued after that Christmas edition.

"In a drear-nighted December
Too happy, happy tree,
Thy branches ne'er remember
Their green felicity."

Above: *An illustration from the December Guide sets the tone for a more relaxed Christmas issue.*

January

Preparation was the watchword for the successful victory gardener in January. Digging over the plot, ordering of seeds, pruning fruit trees and inspecting tools. For the wartime gardener advance preparation was more essential than ever before, as shortages of seeds and fertilisers meant that those who ordered late might find themselves going without.

As the *Allotment & Garden Guide* pointed out '*Before the war many of our seeds came from countries that were until recently under enemy control*'. Whatever seeds you did manage to get hold of, the condition of the soil was essential for good yields. Fortunately, although manure of all types was also hard to come by, the government's official National Growmore Fertiliser had been developed especially to meet the needs of the novice gardener. Available since 1942 it provided a balance of nitrogen, phosphate and potash and despite initial distrust of 'artificials' in the garden, it played an essential part in wartime production.

Gardeners were encouraged to supplement the standard 42lb of Growmore with any organic materials they could get hold of, including constructing a new-fangled compost heap. Hoof, horn, bonemeal and blood were still the gardener's favourites when they could be obtained and were recommended as a winter dressing for fruit trees, helping the many small orchards which had been renovated as part of the war effort.

ALLOTMENT &

Garden Guide

VOL. 1 No. 1   JANUARY · 1945

IN this new series of monthly "Guides" we are out to help you to get better results from your vegetable plot and your fruit garden, Every month we shall try to do three things : first, we shall remind you of the things that ought to have been done, but may not have been possible because of the weather or for some other reason ; secondly, we shall deal with gardening operations for the month ; thirdly, we shall look ahead a month or two and remind you of what you need to do in readiness.

For more detailed week by week information you would do well to take in one of the weekly gardening journals, as soon as the supply situation permits. And your daily or weekly newspaper probably runs a gardening feature that would be helpful to you.

Get ready for
OUTDOOR WORK

January is generally a fairly quiet time in the garden. But you need to push on with your digging and manuring whenever the weather and the state of the land permit. You should also prune and begin to spray your fruit trees, if you have not already done these jobs. But January is a time when you should be thinking and planning, ordering your seed potatoes, vegetable seeds, fertilizers and so on, and making sure that your tools are in good order and that you are ready to begin gardening in real earnest next month, or as soon as local conditions will let you.

Before coming to the various jobs of the month, there is one really important matter that we should say something about—the condition of your soil and the great need to keep it in good heart, for we must not expect to go on producing satisfactory crops year after year unless we restore to the soil what the plants take from it. We must also keep the soil in "good tilth."

What is GOOD TILTH?

It is the top foot or so of soil got into a "crumby" condition. The "crumbs" hold a lot of water on their surfaces and let surplus water drain away quickly through the big pore spaces between them. These spaces supply air, which the roots need as well as water. When rain falls, the uppermost "crumbs" soak it up till they are saturated—like blotting paper dipped in water. Then the surplus soaks downward to the "crumbs" immediately below, and so on. Each "crumb" is like a little sponge. If there is more rain than the "crumbs" can hold, the bigger spaces between them allow the extra water to drain quickly downward and the soil does not become water-logged. The roots of plants in "crumby" soil can grow easily down the air spaces between the "crumbs." All around them are "crumbs" containing the water the roots need. At the tips of the roots are tiny hairs which absorb water. So you will see how important it is that the tips of the roots should not be damaged when planting out.

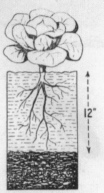

THE VALUE OF HUMUS

What is "humus"? It is a formless material made up of tiny particles produced from the remains of plants and animals when they have decayed. It helps to maintain a "good tilth" and thus ensures good aeration. But it does more; it helps the soil to remain moist and provides plant foods.

~~~~~~~~~~~~~~

'Organic' MANURES

"Organic" manures help to make clay soils lighter and sandy soils better able to hold water. "Organics" are so called because they are formed from something that was living—plants or animals, or both. What are they? The best known are farmyard manure and other animal droppings, such as pig and poultry manure. Other "organic" manures include guano, hoof and horn meal, dried blood, meat and bone meal, shoddy and soot. But market gardeners make great use of these "organics" and it may not be easy for the amateur grower to get them. You yourself can make "organic" manures, either in the form of green manure—a green crop, such as mustard, grown specially for digging in—or compost, which you can make from waste garden material.

THE THREE ESSEN-TIAL PLANT FOODS

"Organic" manures usually provide essential plant foods, the three most important being Nitrogen, Phosphate and Potash. Plants need a balanced ration of these foods. They take them in, dissolved in soil water, through their roots. Most soils contain a certain amount of them. But if the plants are to get enough, you must keep up the supply by manuring the soil. You can do this most effectively by using both "organic" manures and mineral fertilizers—popularly called "artificials".

MANURE IN ROTATION

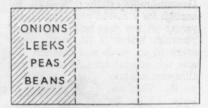

But, you may say, farmyard manure is very scarce and most difficult to get. That is true ; but you can make compost yourself (Dig for Victory Leaflet No. 7 tells you how—it is free), though maybe you could not make enough from your garden waste to supply all the needs of your land in one season. So it is a question of using wisely what little manure you can get or the compost you can make. If you manured about one-third of your land with farmyard manure or compost every year and practised crop rotation (as recommended in the Ministry's free cropping plan), you would go some way to keeping your soil in good heart. The one-third of the plot most suitable for this treatment is the part where you are going to grow your onions, leeks, peas and beans.

About 'Artificials'

Now a word about "artificials"—or, what is a better term, "mineral fertilizers". The use of the word "artificials" makes some people think that "artificials" are not as good as "organics". Both supply exactly the same kind of plant foods in different quantities. The "organics" generally rot down slowly and so supply steady though small amounts of plant foods during the whole of the plant's growing period.

The well-known Sulphate of Ammonia, which comes from gas works and coke ovens, is a good source of nitrogen. Superphosphate, made from rock, is rich in phosphate;

basic slag, which we get from iron works, also contains phosphate. Potash is dug out of mines in France and Germany.

A SOUND GOVERN-MENT FERTILIZER

To meet the needs of gardeners, the Government arranged for the supply of a good standard fertilizer at a reasonable price. It is called "National Growmore Fertilizer" and contains the three important plant foods—the analysis being 7 per cent. N. (nitrogen), 7 per cent. P_2O_5 (phosphate) and 7 per cent. K_2O (potash).

3

On most soils, 42 lb. of National Growmore Fertilizer should be enough for a 10-rod plot (300 square yards). A few days before sowing or planting, scatter 1 lb. evenly over every 10 sq. yards and rake in. To give this general dressing to a 10-rod allotment will take 30 lb. This will leave 12 lb. for giving an extra dressing to potatoes, winter green crops and spring

cabbages. 4½ lb. should be reserved for potatoes and should be applied at planting time. 5½ lb. should be kept for applying during August to the autumn and winter green crops when they are making active growth. The remaining 2 lb. should be used during March as a top dressing for spring cabbage.

You will be able to get National Growmore Fertilizer from most sundries merchants. Allotment societies and similar bodies, which have hitherto bought their fertilizers in bulk, are able to buy National Growmore Fertilizer in bulk at reduced prices.

On some allotments or in some gardens it may be necessary to give an additional top dressing of a nitrogenous fertilizer (such as Sulphate of Ammonia) to any growing crops, applying it at the rate of about 1 lb. per 10 square yards.

The importance of LIME

Lime is of great importance to the garden. Decaying vegetable matter and certain fertilizers tend to make soils acid or "sour". This is bad for plant growth, so lime must be added to make the soil sweet. Do not add too much, for plants grow best in a neutral soil. Lime contains calcium and this is a plant food. Lime or chalk also improves the texture of clay soils, making it easier to get a good tilth.

So do not neglect to lime your land if it needs it ; but do not overdo it. As a general rule the vegetable garden benefits from a dressing of lime every third or fourth year. Lime is particularly good for crops of the cabbage family and helps to control "club root". So lime the part of the plot on which these crops are to be grown. In fact, it is a good plan to lime a third of the plot each year, so that the whole plot will be limed once in three years. Apply the lime after you have finished digging. Do not apply it at the same time as farmyard manure. Fork it in lightly or let it lie on the surface to be washed in by

rain. If you are uncertain whether or not your soil needs lime, ask some knowledgeable person to advise you —your local Parks Superintendent or the County Horticultural Officer at the County Council Offices in your county town.

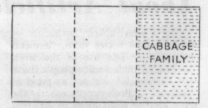

Gardening societies, which bulk their orders so that they amount to not less than 2 tons, can get lime for food production at half price under the Government's Land Fertility Scheme, if the society is registered as an approved association under the scheme. You can get particulars from the Agricultural Lime Department (U.K.) of the Ministry at Hotel Majestic, St. Annes, Lytham St. Annes, Lancs.

REMINDERS

Here are some reminders of the things to do in case you have not already done them.

GET YOUR SEED CATALOGUE

If you want a catalogue, write to your seedsman, for he is still not allowed to send you one unless you do. And order your seed potatoes and vegetable seeds in good time, not just before it is time to put them in—or you may be caught napping.

SEED POTATOES

You can work out the quantity you will need fairly easily if you remember that seed potatoes usually average 5 or 6 tubers to the pound, and that a convenient distance to plant early varieties is a foot apart; other varieties 15 inches apart.

Yields from allotments and gardens are usually less than from an equal area of potatoes on the farm. One important cause is unsatisfactory seed. No amount of manure or good cultivation will make up for the initial disadvantage of poor seed. It is unwise to save for seed potatoes grown in allotments or gardens. So get good seed carrying a "Health"

certificate issued by one of the Agricultural Departments. That is your safeguard. Consult some knowledgeable local grower about this and about the varieties best suited to your district. Here are some selected varieties for your guidance :—

EARLIES

Epicure, Arran Pilot, Sharpe's Express, Duke of York, May Queen, Ninety-Fold.

SECOND EARLIES

Dunbar Rover, Great Scot.

MAINCROPS

Majestic, King Edward VII, Arran Banner, Gladstone, Kerr's Pink, Redskin, Up-to-Date, Arran Victory, Arran Peak, Dunbar Standard.

As soon as you get your seed potatoes, place them in shallow boxes with the crown or rose end upwards, and keep in a cool, dry place with plenty of light, but frost-proof. Make quite sure by covering in severe weather. Sprouting potatoes makes for earliness and high yields. "Dig for Victory" Leaflet No. 12 will give you more detailed information about seed potatoes.

VEGETABLE SEEDS

Seedsmen, like most traders, are working under difficulties due to the war. Before the war many of our seeds came from countries that were until recently under enemy control, and while we can still get most kinds, certain varieties—perhaps your favourites—may be short. If you cannot get just the variety you like, trust your seedsman to supply the nearest to it. If you deal with a reliable firm, you will be safe to leave matters in their hands. But order well in advance of sowing time and give the seedsman every chance to do his best for you. If you are in any doubt about varieties that do well in your district, your seedsman will be able to advise you—or you can consult an experienced neighbour. Estimating your seed requirements is fairly easy, once you have sketched out a rough plan of your plot and worked out the number and length of the rows of each vegetable you intend to have.

One pound of shallots contains about 25 bulbs, and 2 lb. should be about enough for an ordinary allotment row of 30

feet. Half an ounce of turnips or swedes will sow 100 feet. A quarter of an ounce of leek will give enough plants for six or eight rows thirty feet long.

One pint of Longpod broad beans will sow a double row 50 feet long. One pint of Windsor broad beans will sow 40 feet of a double row. Half a pint of French or Haricot beans is sufficient for 150 feet. This enables you to sow 2 seeds every 9 inches to allow for failures.

Half a pint of runner beans will sow one row 50 feet long. One ounce of beet will sow 90 feet of row. Half an ounce of carrot is enough for 100 feet. A small packet or $\frac{1}{4}$ oz. of each variety of lettuce should be enough for successive sowings to give summer and winter supplies. One ounce of onion seed will sow 150 feet—by sowing very thinly you can make it go still further.

Half an ounce of parsnip is enough for 100 feet. One pint of peas will sow 90 feet of row —if you sow very thinly ; for very early sowings you should allow a little more seed, as some may rot if the soil is cold and wet. One ounce of radish will give you all you need.

GET YOUR FERTILIZERS NOW

Make sure of your fertilizers now, so that you will have them at hand when needed. 42 lb. of "National Growmore", the Government approved fertilizer, is enough for a 10-rod (300 sq. yds.) plot, and on page 4 we have told you how to use it.

LOOK AFTER YOUR TOOLS

The wise gardener will examine his tools now and see if any need to be replaced. If so, he will buy them now. Retailers cannot get supplies easily, and if you put off buying until the last minute you may find the tools are not available until it is too late.

A little care is well worth while. Many a tool has had years taken off its useful life by being allowed to rust in a damp shed. No good gardener lets his tools rust, for he knows they take more energy to use when their surfaces are dull.

Here are a few tips for keeping them in first-class order :—

★ Never put your garden tools away dirty. Wash off any soil adhering to them and dry them with an old cloth.

★ Always wipe them over with an oily rag before putting them away.

★ Don't leave them lying about where they may rust or rot.

The best way to keep them in good condition is to use them often.

LOOK AT YOUR STORED CROPS

Inspect all crops you have in store. Potatoes, onions, shallots, carrots, beet and turnips should be looked at every few weeks, just to make certain that they are safe from frost, wet, rats and other enemies, removing any that show the first signs of decay.

Look to your FRUIT TREES & BUSHES

Earlier in this "Guide" we have advised you to prune and spray your fruit trees and bushes before the end of January.

Pruning fruit trees is a complicated job ; if you have never done it you would be well advised to get a friend fairly skilled at the job to prune your trees for you. Watch him carefully while he is doing it and get him to explain why he is making the various cuts, so that you will get to know how to do it yourself. Very often more damage is done by unwise pruning than if the trees were left unpruned, and it is necessary to know a little about the reasons for pruning before starting. Briefly, the aim is to train the tree into a good shape, to prevent it from becoming a tangled mass of branches that would exclude light and air and to encourage the

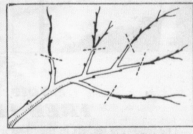

production of fruit buds and regular cropping.

Pruning bush fruits is usually somewhat easier than pruning tree fruits.

You will find "Dig for Victory" Leaflet No. 25 of some help in pruning both trees and bushes. It is illustrated and you can get a free copy from the Ministry at the address given on page 8.

SPRAYING

Nowadays the old-fashioned custom of lime washing fruit trees in the winter has almost disappeared. The modern method of pest control on apples, pears, plums and currants (both black and red) is to spray before the end of January with a tar-oil spray, and later with a lime-sulphur spray, and other washes at various stages of growth.

For the moment, the tar-oil wash is most important. You can buy it almost anywhere with full directions for making up. Remember to choose a dry day (not frosty), with little or no wind, for spraying ; and make sure that all the branches have been thoroughly wetted all over. Cover up any plants under or near the trees or bushes or the spray will damage them. Newspapers will do.

MANURING FRUIT TREES

If apple and pear trees are not growing very strongly, a dressing of 3 or 4 oz. of hoof and horn meal to the square yard, lightly forked into the ground during winter over the area covered by the branches, will encourage them to make strong growth. In addition, one ounce to the square yard of Sulphate of Ammonia should be worked into the surface soil in spring. Apples and pears especially need potash, and dressings of wood ash from the bonfire should be worked into the ground in April. Bone meal is a useful manure for fruit trees, but need only be applied once every three or four years at the rate of about 3 oz. per square yard. Plums too benefit by a similar dressing, but should also have a dressing of 2 oz. of sulphate of ammonia to the square yard each spring.

Some helpful FREE LEAFLETS

The following leaflets in the "Dig for Victory" series are *free* for the asking and may be helpful to you. You can get them by writing to the Ministry of Agriculture at Berri Court Hotel, St. Annes, Lytham St. Annes, Lancs :—

Dig for Victory Leaflet—

No. 1—Cropping Plan for a 10-rod plot (300 sq. yds.).
No. 23—Cropping Plan for a 5-rod plot (150 sq. yds.).
No. 7—How to make a Compost Heap.
No. 12—Seed Potatoes.
No. 18—Better Fruit—Disease Control in Private Gardens.
No. 25—How to Prune Fruit Trees and Bushes.

There are other useful leaflets in the series : send for a list to the above address.

Wt. T17708/8293 50M 12/44 CN&CoLtd.

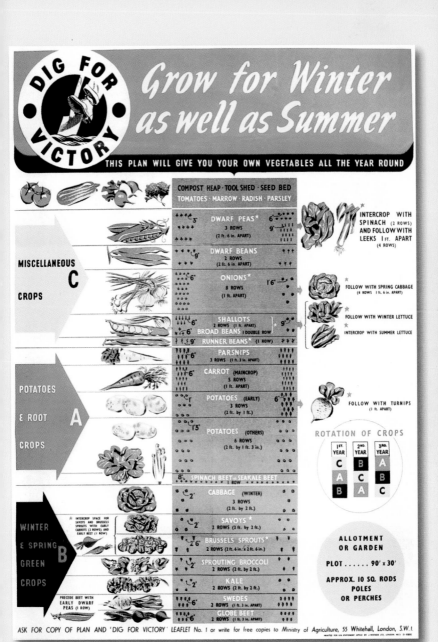

This Dig for Victory leaflet provided advice on ensuring that food would be available year round. (HMSO)

February

For those that had missed the first edition of the *Allotment & Garden Guide* in January, February's edition replayed many of the reminders to order seeds early, prepare the soil and spray the fruit trees. With the first-ever garden centres not due to arrive in England for at least another ten years, gardeners were totally reliant on local nurseries or seedsmen, or mail order catalogues. Catalogues themselves had been in short supply in the previous two years, due both to a high level of demand and shortage of paper.

Many companies charged for their flower seed catalogues, but provided the vegetable catalogues for free as part of the Dig for Victory campaign. However they were not allowed merely to send out the catalogues on the off-chance; the anxious gardener had to write and ask for a catalogue to ensure there was no wastage of precious paper and print.

Still hoping to encourage novice gardeners, even in this sixth year of war, much of February's *Allotment & Garden Guide* was given over to the mysteries of crop rotation. At the outbreak of war less had been made of crop rotation, hinting as it did of the possibility of a long-lasting campaign. However, as the need for better yields became more pressing, crop rotation became an essential art. In the words of the Guide: if your '*wife or whoever runs the kitchen department*' was complaining of lack of vegetables in February, then you needed to try harder! Nowadays crop rotation is second nature to allotment holders and 'the kitchen department' is often a free-for-all!

MINISTRY OF AGRICULTURE

ALLOTMENT &

Garden Guide

VOL. 1 No. 2	**FEBRUARY - 1945**

"FEBRUARY Fill Dyke" may live up to that old country title—or it may not. We shall not be so rash as to prophesy what the weather will be, for though it may be snowing or raining in the North, the South may be basking in the sun—even if a wintry one. However, if the weather be fine in February, we shall be anxious to get on to the vegetable plot ; if it is not, then we can do a bit of thinking and planning indoors. We can profitably take stock of where we stand and make sure that we are ready to start operations as soon as the weather is right and the ground fit.

Never work the soil when it is too wet and sticky and clings in lumps to your boots. You do more harm than good by walking on it and working it when it is like that. And that applies also to sowing seeds, for seeds sown in cold, wet soil will rot instead of germinating, or they will make but poor growth.

If you can settle down to do a bit of thinking and planning—and plotting things out on paper—it will be worth your while to read carefully what is said later about the importance of crop rotation. It may save you a headache in the months ahead if you plan the lay-out of your vegetable plot. And when you do, bear in mind what you have got growing now in the way of vegetables. If you have an abundance and a good selection—and your family eats what you grow—then you won't go far wrong if you stick to last year's plan (rotating your crops, of course). But if your wife, or whoever runs the kitchen department, complains that there is little or nothing in the garden and that shop prices are high, it would pay you to plan so that you grow your own winter vegetables—especially greens. But before you get down to planning, have you yet got or ordered what you will need when you can start outdoor operations? These are the items:

Have you got those SEEDS?

Perhaps, if the weather is suitable, you will be sowing broad beans (unless black fly has broken your heart!) and spinach in February—and planting shallots and Jerusalem artichokes (if you like them). Have you got these items or ordered them? If not, get busy. And if you have planned all you are going to grow this season, order all your requirements right away from your seedsman or nurseryman.

The value of a good strain of seed is tremendous, so deal with a good supplier. And, if you have not already done so, write for his catalogue without delay. You may not be able to get your favourite varieties, but the catalogue will show you what is available, and your supplier will advise you about suitable alternatives to your favourites. And use the order form he supplies: it is more easily dealt with than an order written on odd pieces of paper. Be patient with the seedsman

and don't worry him by constant reminders. He's got his troubles, too.

Don't forget to "Sprout" your Seed Potatoes

If you haven't ordered your seed potatoes, do so at once. As soon as they reach you, set them up to sprout (rose end uppermost) in shallow boxes in a cool (though frost-proof), dry shed, where they can get plenty of light and produce the short, sturdy shoots that make for earliness and high yield. Don't let them get even slightly chilled, for that's enough to kill the "eyes".

USE THIS!

Have you got your NATIONAL GROWMORE FERTILISER?

You will need it for dressing your land before sowing and planting. It contains the three essential plant foods in balanced proportions, and 42lb. is enough for 300 square yards. The January "Guide" explained how it should be used.

OTHER REMINDERS

Finally, see that your tools are in good condition for use. When you start outdoors you will need a line for straightness and pegs to mark the rows. And you would find a 6-ft. rod, marked off in 6 in. and 3 in. sections, very useful.

And continue to have a look at your stored crops to see that there is no damage or decay. Rub off any potato sprouts on your eating crop in store. Lift any outdoor parsnips to check growth, storing them under protection at the north side of a fence or wall, if you can.

/\/\/\/\/\/\/\/\

CROP ROTATION is most important

Some gardening beginners have no doubt been puzzled by the term "crop rotation." It sounds a bit mysterious, but it is really quite simple. And it is the only sound basis for vegetable growing. To be a successful gardener you must be methodical. What does "crop rotation" mean? Simply arranging your cropping in such a way as to avoid growing the same kinds of crops on any section of your plot one year after another. To grow the same crop on the same ground year after year is bad gardening for several reasons. There is also the risk that diseases and pests will be increased in the soil to attack again the following year. Rotation of vegetable crops affects the condition of your land in four important ways.

★ It ensures that every part of your plot carries, at regular intervals, crops that require thorough soil cultivation.

★ It helps to maintain the content of plant food and humus in all parts of the plot. Some crops will repay for heavier dressings of fertilisers than others, and some will get what farmyard manure or compost is available.

★ It helps to control weeds, for different crops need different cultivations at different seasons; though weeds may withstand the appropriate cultivations for one crop, they may be kept down by the cultivations for another crop.

★ It helps to control pests and diseases.

The Ministry of Agriculture recommends a three-year "crop rotation" for a 300 sq. yd. plot, and its official cropping plan, which is free for the asking, has enjoyed a wide circulation. It was not intended that gardeners should follow it slavishly, for what suits one part of the country does not suit another. And people have different tastes in vegetables. The Ministry's plan aims at two important things—crop rotation and a sufficiency of vegetables throughout the year, especially in winter when so many gardens still show the scarcity of crops that results from poor planning.

The right approach for the gardener is, first to find out what vegetables grow satisfactorily in his neighbourhood, and then decide which of them he will grow, bearing in mind his family's likes and dislikes. He should then divide his plot into three equal parts. For simplicity we will call them A, B and C. On plot A he will grow the first year potatoes and other roots—parsnips (if his family like them), carrots, beet and so on. On plot B he will grow green vegetables — all the cabbage family ; and on plot C he will grow peas, beans, onions and leeks.

If farmyard manure is difficult to get (it is in most districts) and the gardener has to eke out the compost we hope he has made, he should manure each year only on the section that is to grow peas, beans, onions and leeks. So in three years the whole plot will be manured.

Now what happens to the plan the second year ? He should just move his three groups round. On plot A, go the peas and beans, onions, etc. ; on plot B, the potatoes and root crops and on plot C, the green vegetables.

1st YEAR	2nd YEAR	3rd YEAR
A POTATOES AND OTHER ROOT CROPS	PEAS BEANS ONIONS LEEKS	CABBAGES SAVOYS BRUSSELS SPROUTING BROCCOLI KALE
B CABBAGES SAVOYS BRUSSELS SPROUTING BROCCOLI KALE	POTATOES AND OTHER ROOT CROPS	PEAS BEANS ONIONS LEEKS
C PEAS BEANS ONIONS LEEKS	CABBAGES SAVOYS BRUSSELS SPROUTING BROCCOLI KALE	POTATOES AND OTHER ROOT CROPS

In the third year he should move them round again—on plot A, the green vegetables ; on plot B, the peas, beans, onions and leeks ; and on plot C, the potatoes and root crops. Then, in the fourth year, he will begin the rotation all over again.

By this simple system you not only ensure that the ground is kept in reasonably fertile condition all over, but it helps you to gauge how much ground you should devote to the various kinds of crops. The rotation can be worked equally well in the garden as on an allotment, but in each case space must be left somewhere

at one end (say, 6 foot wide) for the seed bed, marrow bed, compost heap and so on.

It is much easier to arrange a proper rotation when starting from scratch ; but even a garden that was worked last year could be brought into line by remembering where your crops were last season and trying to plant the appropriate vegetables this year to follow them up.

Crop rotation will help with liming, too, if your soil needs lime. It is a good idea to lime each year that part of the plot that carried potatoes and root vegetables the year before.

Now for the jobs you can do outdoors in February, if the weather is "open" and the soil workable. Don't forget to rake in a good general fertiliser, such as "National Growmore", a few days before sowing or planting.

5

Sow *BROAD BEANS*

The earliest and often most successful crops of broad beans are obtained by sowing in autumn (but not in the North, unless protected by frames or cloches) : but a second

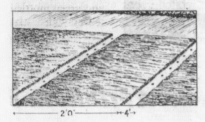

← 2'0" → ←4'→

sowing can be made during February. The broad bean does best on land manured for a previous crop, such as potatoes.

It is best to sow two lines of seed to each row, with 6 in. between the seeds and 2 ft. 6 in. between the rows. But if only one line of seeds is sown, 2 ft. between rows will be sufficient.

Sow 2 in. deep in holes made with a dibber, dropping one good seed in each hole. Or make a flat-bottomed drill 2 in. deep. Space the seed out 6 in. apart.

Sow *SPINACH*

The Ministry's cropping plan suggests that summer spinach (for those who like it) should be sown in mid-April. But if you wish, you can make successional sowings from February to May in drills 1 in. deep and 12 in. apart. Thin out the plants as soon as they are large enough to handle, first to 3 in. apart, removing alternate plants about a fortnight later. You can cook these thinnings. On light soils spinach runs to seed fairly quickly in hot weather, so hoe regularly and water freely at such times, if you can.

Spinach likes well manured ground.

FIRST THINNING

← 3" →

SECOND THINNING (After fortnight)

← 6" →

Plant *SHALLOTS*

Shallots are easier to grow than onions and some gardeners prefer them for that reason ; in fact, shallots are a sort of hardy perennial onion grown annually from small bulbs or "sets". You can also grow shallots from seed, but these bulbs are really small onions and are useless for replanting and should be used up each year.

The Ministry's cropping plan for a 300 square yard plot suggests two rows of shallots to be planted in February. Sets of medium size (20 to 25 to the lb.) should be used and each set should produce five or six large bulbs. 2 lb. of bulbs should be about enough for one row of 30 ft.

Plant in rows 1 ft. apart and 6 in. or 9 in. between the bulbs, leaving the top of each bulb just showing above soil level. Crops are usually mature by early July and should be taken up, carefully dried and stored.

Save, for re-planting, sufficient *medium-sized* bulbs from strong,

healthy plants (mark them with a stick during the growing season). Avoid using bulbs from plants that have made but poor growth and may show yellow and green mottled leaves which suggest virus disease.

Plant Jerusalem Artichokes

While the Ministry's plan does not suggest artichokes, your family may like them. And if you keep poultry or rabbits they will like them, too. Another good point is that you can grow artichokes in any odd corner, and they can be useful to screen a shed or the manure or compost heap. Though they can put up with rougher conditions than most vegetables, they will repay for good cultivation.

You can plant artichoke tubers in February or March in drills 6 in. deep. Set the tubers 12 in. to 15 in. apart, leaving 2 ft. 6 in. between rows. When the plants appear, hoe between them and draw the soil towards them. You cut the tall stalks down in early winter, leaving the tubers in the ground and lifting

as you need them. Keep a number of tubers for replanting to provide a supply for the following year. Though artichokes are perennial and can be left in the ground several years, it is well to lift and replant a section every year so that the land doesn't get weedy or overcrowded.

Do you grow RHUBARB?

If you do, February or March, when growth is starting, is the time to divide old roots, using a sharp spade or knife, and cutting so that each piece contains at least one or two good buds. Rhubarb likes deeply-dug and well-manured ground (use com-

post if you cannot get manure), for the plants usually have to stay put for several years.

Plant in a sunny spot about 2 ft. apart, and do not pull any of the stalks from plants divided this year.

7

Get ready for "RUNNERS"

Though you will not be sowing your "runners" until, say, mid-May, now is the time to get the ground prepared for them, if it is not already. They need good cultivation and do best when grown where the soil is trenched and dressed with a good dressing of well-rotted manure or compost. So if you have not manured the particular plot where your beans are to go, take out a trench a spit deep, work in a liberal dressing of manure or compost into the lower spit and then replace the top spit.

Remember, when ordering your seeds, that half-a-pint of runner beans will sow a row 50 ft. long.

SOME USEFUL PUBLICATIONS

The Ministry of Agriculture has published during the war a number of free leaflets and priced publications that may be helpful to you, if you have not already had them. There are still some stocks of the "Dig for Victory" leaflets which you can get free from the Ministry at

Berri Court Hotel, St. Annes, Lytham St. Annes, Lancs. You can get the bulletins through any bookseller or direct from H.M. Stationery Office, York House, Kingsway, W.C.2., at the prices mentioned below.

Here are some topical leaflets :—

DIG FOR VICTORY LEAFLETS

No. 1—Cropping Plan for a 10-rod plot (300 sq. yards)

No. 23—Cropping Plan for a 5-rod plot (150 sq. yards)

No. 2—Onions and related crops

No. 4—Peans and Beans

No. 7—How to make a Compost Heap

No. 12—Seed Potatoes

No. 19—How to sow Seeds

And here are some suggestions for priced bulletins :—

"Growmore" Bulletins

No. 1—Food from the Garden —3d. (4d.)

No. 2—Pests and Diseases in the Vegetable Garden— 4d. (5d.)

No. 3—Preserves from the Garden—4d (5d.)

No. 7—Fruit from the Garden —3d. (4d.)

The prices are net ; those in brackets include postage.

Wt. T.20173/8500 50M 2/45 7/4 CN&Co Ltd

HOW TO SOW SEEDS

DIG FOR VICTORY LEAFLET
NUMBER 19 (NEW SERIES)

ISSUED BY THE MINISTRY OF AGRICULTURE

Small guides were also produced covering some of the very basic gardening techniques such as this one, Number 19 'How To Sow Seeds', mentioned opposite. (HMSO)

March

With a pressing need to provide crops as early as possible, March was greeted with enthusiastic seed sowing. Brussels sprouts, leeks, parsnips, peas, lettuces, radishes, parsley and potatoes joined the broad beans, spinach, shallots and Jerusalem artichokes that had already been planted or sown in February.

Onion seed should already have been sown under glass in January or February, but could now be sown outdoors. Before the war over 90 per cent of onions had been imported from France and Spain, and few gardeners had bothered to grow their own. Onions were considered a difficult crop, needing careful sowing and transplanting out, and then continuous weeding. The seed itself was considered 'fickle' taking at least three weeks to come up even in good conditions, and then with only patchy germination.

Shallots, planted as small bulbs, were a more popular crop and easier to grow. Modern gardeners use these 'sets' or small bulbs for onions as well as shallots and rarely bother with onion seed. The importance given to onions during the war can be gauged from the official recommendation that eight rows of onions should be sown, just one row less than the nine rows of that other essential crop, the potato. However, many people found onions too strong in taste, preferring the milder shallot. Anyone using artificial fertiliser since decimalisation would be wise to substitute a 50p piece for the penny shown on page 3!

MINISTRY OF AGRICULTURE

ALLOTMENT
AND
Garden Guide

VOL. 1 No. 3   MARCH - 1945

"March winds and April showers,
Bring forth the May flowers."

That was a peace-time couplet. "Not yet must the flowers invade the fat green hinterland of the war-time allotment", a Northern newspaper recently declared. As it pointed out, fresh allotment produce—garden stuff, too—is going to be of immense value during the first few years after the war, when there will be a great strain upon road, rail and all transport. The man who can grow his own produce on his own plot will not only be making an important contribution to a smooth transition from war to peace, but will also be looking after his own family interests best.

The Ministry does not rule out flowers altogether. As the Northern newspaper happily put it : "Now and again an allotment holder will disinterestedly set himself to cheer us all up by bedding out—in true peace-time parkland style—with lobelias, geraniums, pansies —just a happy fringe of them along the hem of his plot." The Ministry itself has said, in effect, that not more than one-tenth of peace-time flowers should be grown, but the paper puts it better with its phrase "just a happy fringe", adding "But behind this gay facade wholesome

"Just a happy fringe..."

produce grows in abundance". And March is the month when gardeners really begin to get busy putting their plans into effect and starting work to produce this wholesome abundance. Now, abundance in summer is easy, *but sufficiency in winter—especially late winter and early spring—is* another kettle of fish. Too many gardeners still fall down on winter production, due to lack of planning. Your local Parks Superintendent or your local allotment or horticultural society may have produced a plan that suits local conditions and makes adequate provision for winter vegetables. Or you can still get the Ministry's cropping plan, not to follow it blindly, but to use it as a guide that you can adapt to meet your family's likes and dislikes and modify in the light of your knowledge of the kinds of vegetables that can be grown satisfactorily in your neighbourhood. And it may be worth your while re-reading what was said in the February issue of this "Guide" about the importance of crop rotation.

Any week now, when weather and soil are right, you will want to start

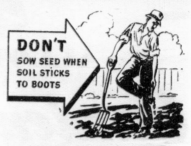

sowing and planting. But one word of warning : don't try to sow seed when the soil sticks to your boots. Wait for a fine spell. When it is fine and the soil is workable, you will perhaps be making successional sowings of broad beans and spinach as described in the February "Guide". You will also be sowing seeds of Brussels sprouts and leeks—both in a special seedbed ; parsnips, peas, onions, lettuces, radishes and parsley —where they are to grow on. And you may also be planting autumn-sown onions.

~~~~~~~~~~~~~~~~

But before getting down to detailed advice on sowing and planting, here are a few brief *reminders* that may not come amiss.

UPROOT THOSE STUMPS

Clear away those old stumps of Brussels, cabbage and so on and get the land prepared for another crop.

SEEDS You have no doubt already got the seeds of the vegetables just mentioned—also your seed potatoes, which should have been "sprouted" ; but during April and May you may be sowing beet, carrots and turnips, as well as runner beans (perhaps French and Haricots too), kales, savoys, cabbages and spinach beet. Marrows must not be overlooked either, if your family likes them. Make sure you get all the seeds in time.

FERTILISER You have probably got a supply of a suitable fertiliser containing the three necessary plant foods—nitrogen, potash, phosphorus—with which to dress your land before sowing and planting. If you haven't, "National Growmore Fertiliser"—a Government recommended product—would suit your needs. 42 lb. will be enough for a 300 square yard plot. The January "Guide" described how to use it.

STICKS AND STAKES

In April you will be sticking your peas, in June your runners. If you intend to grow tomatoes, you will need stakes for them at the end of May when you plant out. Have you got your sticks and stakes or ordered them ?

FEED SPRING CABBAGE

In the January "Guide" it was recommended that out of the 42 lb. of "National Growmore Fertiliser" that you might buy, you should set aside 2 lb. as a top dressing for spring cabbage. Or you can use sulphate of ammonia, applying it at the rate of one ounce per yard run. Lettuces and spinach would also benefit by a similar application. But keep the fertiliser off the leaves.

LIFT LEEKS
If you grew leeks last season and need the land on which they stand, for other crops, lift the remaining plants and heel them in in a shady spot. In any case, it is not wise to leave leeks too long in their rows.

GETTING THE "ROOT" GROUND READY
As soon as it becomes free, dig over the land you intend for your root crops. Leave it rough until you are ready to sow. In April you can break it down and lightly fork in a dressing of 1 lb. of "National Growmore Fertiliser" to every 10 square yards.

GUIDES FOR ESTIMATING WEIGHT OF FERTILISER

½ OZ — PENNY

2 OZ — TABLESPOON

Now for SOWING & PLANTING

Some seeds are best sown in a seedbed—for instance cabbage, kales, sprouts, sprouting broccoli and leeks ; others, such as the root crops and lettuces, are usually sown where they are to remain. As you may be sowing Brussels sprouts and leeks during March, let us first say something about

How to use a SEEDBED

Here are the essential points :—

★ Mark off a patch about 6 ft. by 4 ft. for a 300 square yard allotment or garden. Break down all lumps during a dry spell and remove any stones and all roots of grass or weeds.

★ Make the soil firm by treading it as soon as it is dry enough not to stick to your boots. Don't stamp it down.

★ Loosen top surface by lightly raking. Place short sticks to mark ends of rows, which should be 4 ft. long across the bed and 6 in. apart. Stretch line between sticks.

★ Stand on a board so as not to tread ground too hard, and make shallow drill along line with label or stick.

★ Sow an even single line of seed along bottom of drill. Cover seed lightly with soil. A good way is to

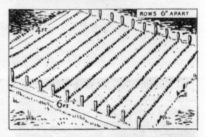

MAKING DRILL

shuffle slowly along with a foot on either side of the drill, and without raising the feet slide the soil back and lightly press it. On heavy soil you may find it easier to scatter fine soil into the drill instead. Rake lightly to finish.

COVERING SEED

Here are two March items for the seedbed :—

BRUSSELS SPROUTS

A small packet of seed is enough for each of the cabbage family. Seed may be sown in seedbed drills about 1½ in. deep—1 ft. apart—from third week in March to end of April. Sow thinly, allowing ⅛ in. between each seed. To protect seedlings from birds use black cotton or wire guards and do it immediately after sowing.

LEEKS Sow thinly in mid-March in shallow seedbed drills.

Here are several items for sowing in March on the actual site where the crops will grow :—

PARSNIPS may be sown from mid-February to mid-March. The Ministry's cropping plan (300 square yards) provides for three rows. Soil for parsnips should always be deeply dug and worked to a fine surface tilth before sowing. Sow in drills 15 in. apart and 1 in. deep, dropping the seed in small clusters of three or four, 6 in. apart. Thin seedlings of each cluster so as to leave only one.

SEED

THIN EACH CLUSTER TO ONE

PEAS The Ministry's plan provides for three rows of dwarf peas 2 ft. 6 in. apart. In view of the difficulty of getting pea sticks, dwarf and medium varieties are most suitable for the garden or allotment, since they can be supported by fewer sticks or by string stretched between short sticks inserted at intervals either side of the row.

If mice are troublesome, before sowing shake the seed in a tin containing a little red lead or paraffin.

NEVER SOW PEAS IN WET SOIL
Wait until it is just nicely moist and works freely. Sow in broad, flat drills from 2 to 2½ in. deep, made with either draw-hoe or spade. Don't just scatter the

3" APART EACH WAY

seeds slapdash in the drill : set them out in three rows (as illustrated) allowing about 3 in. each way between seeds. This may sound unnecessarily finicky, but it is worth it and the job takes only a few extra minutes.

Space the rows according to the height of variety, 2 ft. for dwarfs, 3 ft. for medium and 5 ft. for tall.

Birds will attack the germinating seeds as they come up, so protect the rows with black cotton stretched on sticks about 6 in. above soil. Or you can use pea guards.

LETTUCE (Summer). Begin in March to sow very thinly in drills, half a row at a time, ½ in. deep, the rows being 1 ft. apart. Continue to sow at fortnightly intervals until July. March-sown lettuces attract slugs, so lime the surface as a deterrent.

Thin the seedlings when the first pairs of true leaves are well formed. The final distance apart should be from 9 to 12 in.

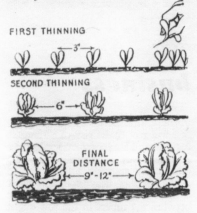

FIRST THINNING

SECOND THINNING

FINAL DISTANCE
9"-12"

RADISHES If you like radishes, you can make a small sowing in March (½ in. deep) and follow up with sowings about every three weeks until May, to keep up a continuous supply.

PARSLEY Make a sowing of parsley in March (½ in. deep) and a second sowing in July for succession. Thin seedlings to 3 to 4 in. apart.

ONIONS The Ministry's cropping plan provides for eight rows of onions. There are three ways of growing them for storage :—

(1) by sowing seed under glass or in warm frames in January and February, and transplanting in April ;

(2) by sowing seed in the open in February or March ;

(3) by sowing in early autumn and transplanting in March.

By sowing in boxes, seed can be made to yield the maximum number of plants. The second method is popular and can be freely practised almost anywhere ; but where soils are difficult to work or onion fly is troublesome, the other methods are recommended.

The onion bed must always be carefully prepared whatever method you use. Soil should have been dug early (before Christmas) and manured liberally. Firmness of soil is essential.

Early sowing is also important, a n d the bed should be prepared as soon as soil is dry enough to work in Feb-

9" TO 12

ruary or March, that is, when it does not stick to the boots. Tread it both ways and rake level, removing all large stones. The seed drills should be drawn 9 to 12 in. apart and about 1 in. deep. Sow seed fairly thinly and evenly and cover it with earth with the feet or back of rake. The soil requires to be gently consolidated by another light treading or by using a light roller.

Onion seed is rather fickle ; it may germinate well or badly, and quickly or slowly according to weather conditions ; but 1 oz. of seed should be sufficient for at least 100 feet. As a rule, it takes about three weeks to come up. It is a good plan to mix with it a little

(PLANTS 6" APART IN ROW FOR LARGE ONIONS)

radish seed; this will germinate quickly and mark the rows, making it possible to cultivate and weed between them before the slower germinating onions come through, when the radishes can be pulled for salad.

Autumn-sown onions should be transplanted in early March on to the prepared onion bed. Plant (see illustration) in rows 1 ft. apart with about 6 in. between plants (for large onions).

~~~~~~~~~~~~~~~

This POTATO business

Throughout the war the Ministry has been consistent in its advice that the household grower should not overdo potatoes (as many are apt to do), that he should not aim at self-sufficiency in this crop unless he has enough ground to allow him first to grow green crops—salads, summer vegetables and, above all, enough winter greens and root crops for his family. "Follow the official cropping plan" has all along been the advice given. And that plan provides for three 30 ft. rows of "earlies" and six 30 ft. rows of main crops for a 300 square yard plot. On plots half that size or less the Ministry considers it would be unwise to use any of the space for main crop potatoes, though two rows of "earlies" might be grown. The limited room in small gardens would be better used for growing green winter vegetables.

PLANTING EARLY
POTATOES If possible, all potato planters—great and small—should "sprout" their seed potatoes before planting, as advised in the previous issues of this "Guide". In any year it is a useful thing to do before planting, because it makes for a larger yield and brings the crop to maturity some weeks earlier.

If you have sprouted your seed potatoes, there is no need to be in a hurry about planting them out. Wait for favourable conditions. With unsprouted seed, however, it is important that the first sprouts, which are the most vigorous, should be formed

in the soil rather than in the bag, for this will reduce the risk of damage in handling. This means early planting. A simple way of planting is to take out shallow trenches 2 ft. apart and 4-5 in. deep on heavy soil, and about 6 in. on light land. The distance between the tubers in the row ought to be not less than 12 in. (15 in. for maincrops).

Heavier crops will be secured by using fertilisers. For gardens and allotments "National Growmore" fertiliser is most convenient. It contains nitrogen, phosphorus and potash—the three important plant foods. The

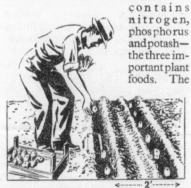

method is to give a dressing of 1 lb. per 10 sq. yards, forked in before planting. Also sow in the drills before planting a light dressing at the rate of 1 lb. per 60 ft. Tubers should not be dusted with artificials, as the eye or sprout may be damaged.

Don't apply lime to cultivated soil in the same season in which it is proposed to crop it with potatoes.

FOOD FOR YOUR GARDEN FROM YOUR GARDEN

The importance of compost was dealt with in the January "Guide". Now it is proposed to tell you what you can use to make it and how to make it—in pictures.

WHAT YOU CAN USE

Leaves, grass cuttings, straw sods, lawn mowings, haulms of peas, beans and potatoes, vegetable tops, hedge clippings, weeds, and faded flowers. In fact, any plant refuse not needed for stock feeding.

WHAT YOU CAN'T USE

Cinders, paper, coal ashes, thick woody stems, sawdust, and any materials tainted with oil, creosote, tar or with any poisonous chemical. Avoid cabbage roots affected by 'club-root' disease.

Make a COMPOST HEAP this way

1. Choose site, in shade if possible, on ground not used for cropping. Width 4-7 ft. Length depends on amount of material available.

2. Cover with layer of vegetable refuse (the more mixed and broken up the better) to 6-9 in. depth. If dry, moisten and tread down well. If green and sappy, lay loosely.

3. (*Left*) Cover with 2 in. layer of animal manure (horse, cow, pig, poultry, pigeon, rabbit) or sewage sludge.   3. (*Right*) If animal manure is not available, sprinkle with one of the special proprietary chemicals or with sulphate of ammonia.

4. Repeat layers 2 and 3 until heap is 3-5 ft. high. If more material is to be dealt with, start a new heap.

5. Sprinkle a little lime, ground limestone or chalk, after every foot or so, or apply layer of chalky soil about 2 in. thick. But if using chemicals, follow maker's directions about lime.

6. When heap has cooled down, turn it over from one end to the other, so that the outside material goes to the middle and that from the middle to the outside.

7

Things to do in the FRUIT GARDEN

Fruit trees benefit by a spring application of 1 oz. of sulphate of ammonia per square yard, worked into the surface soil in spring. And if you are having garden bonfires in March, don't forget to keep the wood ash in a dry place. Apples and pears need the potash the wood ash contains, so work the ash into the soil in April.

Plum trees, too, benefit from a dressing of 2 oz. of sulphate of ammonia to the square yard in spring.

Early in April you may have to spray your blackcurrants, if they are troubled with "big bud".

Lime sulphur is the spray for this and you can get it ready made up with full directions for use.

Gooseberries also should be sprayed in April with lime sulphur, to ward off mildew before the flowers appear.

Apples (except "Beauty of Bath," "Stirling Castle" and "St. Cecilia") may be sprayed with lime sulphur while still in the green bud stage, that is, when the green flower buds are visible but have not begun to turn colour. This treatment will protect against "scab," but should be repeated during April when the trees are at the "pink bud" stage, that is, *before* the flower buds begin to open, but after they have begun to show colour.

~~~~~~~~~~~~~~~~

SOME PUBLICATIONS *that may help you*

If you would like more information about compost making than this "Guide" gives you, you would find this leaflet provides it—"Dig for Victory" Leaflet No. 7—"How to make a Compost Heap". As disease control in the fruit garden has been touched on, you may also like to get No. 18—"Better Fruit—Disease Control in Private Gardens".

All these leaflets are free, and you can get them by dropping a post-card to the Ministry at Berri Court Hotel, St. Annes, Lytham St. Annes, Lancashire.

The April "Guide" will touch on some pests of the vegetable garden. One of the Ministry's bulletins, "Pests and Diseases in the Vegetable Garden" deals more fully with the subject and if you have not already got it you may like to know where it is obtainable. It costs 4d. (post free 5d.) and you can get it through any bookseller or direct from H.M. Stationery Office, York House, Kingsway, L'don. W.C.2

8

HOME-GROWN FOOD

MARCH TO APRIL ISSUE

WHAT TO GROW
BY THE MINISTRY OF AGRICULTURE

HOW TO COOK IT
BY FREDDIE GRISEWOOD
(Of the B.B.C. Kitchen Front)

The Minister of Agriculture, the Rt. Hon. R. S. HUDSON, M.P., sends this special message to you :—

"Your family—especially the children—must eat vegetables to keep them fit. Green vegetables are vital to their winter health. It is up to you—women as well as men—to see they get them. Don't rely on others. Our farmers are doing their utmost to give you milk, bread, potatoes and other vital food. That is their main job, but you can make sure of getting enough vegetables too by growing your own. If you have a garden, turn it over to vegetables. If you have no garden, ask your local Council for an allotment."

Leaflets were also produced to show housewives how to cook the abundance of green vegetables that they had produced. The Ministry of Agriculture and Ministry of Food co-ordinated their efforts.

April

'Friend or Foe?' was a constant refrain of the war years. For the gardener that meant being able to identify the huge range of beetles and bugs that inhabited the vegetable patch. Chemical sprays were increasingly common amongst the weaponry of the 'Allotment Army', but traditional gardeners still preferred to pick off caterpillars and make their own slug traps. For the novice gardener, correct identification was the first round in the battle against the pests.

Letters in the gardening press of the period suggest that aphid eaters such as ladybirds and centipedes were often confused with the pests they helped to reduce. The *Allotment & Garden Guide* made the recognition of the friendly centipede easier by equipping him with a Union Jack, while the millipede was weighted down by a Swastika. Hopefully the garden reader realised that in real life identification might be trickier.

Nationalism was also apparent in the blame attached to the flocks of non-native cabbage white butterflies that apparently swarmed in from the continent every year to lay their eggs on brassicas. Biological methods of pest control were still many years in the future in 1945, although hand picking and drowning caterpillars was a task allotted to many children.

Anxious to keep gardeners at it, the Ministry of Agriculture continuously played down the prospects of peace fearing that abandonment of allotments would result in widespread starvation.

MINISTRY OF AGRICULTURE

ALLOTMENT

AND

Garden Guide

VOL. 1 No. 4   APRIL - 1945

> "April, April,
> Laugh thy girlish laughter ;
> Then, the moment after,
> Weep thy girlish tears."

IF April lives up to that reputation, she will please readers of this Guide, though we shall look to her to be judicious in her weeping. We shall want useful spells of sunny weather throughout this busy gardening month. But let us sound a word or two of warning. Good Friday is the traditional day for potato planting ; but the wise gardener knows that it's risky to stick to traditions : he pays more attention to soil and weather conditions. And although we shall be only too anxious to get on with arrears of clearing up, digging, seed sowing and planting, we shall find that "hasten slowly" is still sound advice when soil conditions are not right.

Getting on with the job

But once weather and soil are right, we should take time by the forelock and get on with the job—not leaving everything to the week-end, if we can help it, but seizing any opportunity of an evening—when it's fine—to put in a little time on essential work on the plot. Little and often will help us along far better than crowding a lot into the week-end that may turn out wet. But, of course, we may yet be far off from those happy, free peace-time evenings.

DON'T DELAY THINNING

In Spring, though, many little jobs come along that need to be done when the time is right. A few days' delay may spoil things : thinning seedlings, for instance ; a wet week-end makes the young seedlings romp away. More about thinning next month.

HOE OFTEN

April is certainly the time for using the Dutch hoe regularly and often. Hoe freely—just the surface, not deeply—between all growing crops and on vacant ground on every favourable occasion. Try, if you can, to move all ground at least every ten days when growth is active, so as to maintain a loose surface mulch and keep down weeds.

Now here are some reminders for this month :—

REMINDERS

In the first three issues of this "Guide" you were reminded about getting all your seeds in good time—your fertilisers, too, as well as pea and bean sticks. One "seed" item not so far mentioned is *swedes.* Though you can sow swedes as early as April, the Ministry's cropping plan, which suggests two rows, recommends sowing in June. Swedes are often successful in districts where it is not so easy to grow carrots, and the field varieties resist the cold better than turnips. Swedes are usually sown in mid-June in the south, though in the north they may be safely sown earlier. More will be said about swedes in a later Guide.

PRESS FIRM

Have a look at your *shallots.* You may have planted them a little too loosely and the weathering may have left them almost bare of soil. Firm them in now.

Now a word or two about *tomatoes.* Of course, you won't think of planting them out until the end of May or the first week in June ; but if you have not done so, you would be wise to put in your order for plants with a reliable supplier. Be warned : don't buy plants that you see for sale much earlier than they should be. You will be disappointed if you buy them.

And what about Brussels sprouts ? These need a long period of growth. If you have not sown seeds in the seedbed and you intend growing them, you should order your plants so that you are not caught napping when you want to plant them out in May or June. And now is the time, if you have not already done so, to clear away those old *cabbage and other green stumps* that may be taking up ground that should be cleared and dug over ready for a following crop. For one thing, these old stumps harbour pests ; but, even more important, if you let them stop until they flower, you may well do harm by cross-pollination to the crops of the professional man who is growing them for valuable seed.

*   *   *

Now for the seed-sowing jobs of the month, remembering that a few days before sowing or planting (except on the seed bed) 1 lb. of a good complete fertiliser—"National Growmore" for instance—should be scattered evenly over every 10 sq. yds. and raked in.

BEANS
DWARF AND HARICOT

The Ministry's cropping plan provides for two rows of dwarfs. The plants of dwarfs are tender and should not be sown in the open until mid-April in the south and mid-May in the north. Successive batches can be sown until mid-July. Rows should be 2 ft. or $2\frac{1}{2}$ ft. apart, with 9 in. between plants. Use a dibber, or draw a shallow trench with a hoe, about 2 in. deep. If you put two seeds at each interval you can reckon on a regular stand. Pull out the unwanted weaker plant, when sufficiently advanced. A light mulching of the surface with lawn mowings, decayed leaves or compost will help to keep the plants growing.

If you grow haricots for storing, you proceed as for dwarfs, but you don't pick any green pods. How you deal with them will be dealt with in a later Guide.

BEET

The official cropping plan provides for two rows of Globe Beet. The globe variety matures quickly and is suitable for general cultivation. It is easier to boil in the usual kitchen pot than the longer varieties—a point that the missus will appreciate. Sow globe crops in April, longer varieties in May. Drills should be $1\frac{1}{2}$ to 2 in. deep and at least 1 ft. apart. Sow seeds in small clusters 6 in. apart, to avoid waste, and thin the plants to one when three leaves have formed. A few strands of black cotton stretched above the rows will protect the seedlings from troublesome birds.

CABBAGES

The Ministry's cropping plan does not include cabbages for use in summer and early autumn, except as an alternative to runner beans in cold districts. If you have enough room, however, and you would like a choice of green vegetables in late summer, sow a row now in the seedbed (see page 3 of March Guide).

CARROTS

The first sowing of carrots—a stump-rooted kind—(to provide roots for summer and autumn) should be made in early April. The storage crop is best sown in May or early June. If sown early, thinnings may be pulled and used as early carrots without harming the rest of the crop ; but the ground must be made firm again after thinning out, to reduce the danger of carrot fly attack. A late sowing in mid-July will provide tender young carrots for use the following spring (April—May).

Sow seed thinly in drills drawn 1 ft. apart and 1 in. deep. As carrot seed is small, mix a little dry earth or sand to avoid too thick sowing, which wastes seed and means a good deal of thinning. First thin in the seedling stage and keep the bed free from weeds by frequent use of the hoe. Plants should finally be 6 in. apart.

LETTUCE

Continue to sow a short row ($\frac{1}{2}$ in. deep) every fortnight, to make sure of crops in succession. (See March Guide, page 4).

PEAS

The March Guide (page 4) dealt with the sowing of peas. This is just to remind you to sow maincrop peas in April. For late crops you can sow such varieties as Little Marvel and Onward as late as June. Unless your soil is in very good heart, a top dressing of superphosphate—2 ounces per square yard—at blossom time helps the pods to swell.

PEAS READY FOR "STICKING"

As soon as the peas begin to make their third pair of leaves, they will be ready for sticking. Even dwarf peas do better with a little support— a few twigs are all that is necessary. Before sticking, hoe the ground beside the rows and remove any weed seedlings showing between the plants, as they will be more difficult to get at when the sticks are in. Don't cross the two rows of sticks at the top, as this usually makes the plants get tangled in a mass ; stick them firmly in the ground—upright. Trim the tops and put the twiggy trimmings in at the bottom by the larger sticks, so that the young plants can grasp them first before climbing on to the sticks.

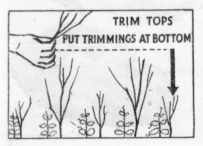

TRIM TOPS
PUT TRIMMINGS AT BOTTOM

POTATOES

Potato planting was dealt with in the March Guide (page 6). April is the month for planting varieties other than "earlies".

RADISHES

Don't forget to sow them little and often, if you like them. Sow very thinly and there will be no need to thin the seedlings. A useful idea is to sow a few radish seeds in the drills along with onions, carrots and beet. Plant one seed every 6 in. or so along the drills ; they grow quickly and show you the line of the drill before the other seeds germinate. Hoeing and weeding can then begin earlier.

SPINACH

The Ministry's cropping plan provides for inter-cropping three rows of dwarf peas with two rows of spinach, if you like it. Gardeners on light soils, however, find that summer spinach runs to seed so quickly unless they kept it well watered.

Some wartime gardeners may be a bit confused yet about spinach, spinach beet and seakale beet. Spinach may be sown both in spring (March to May) and late summer (August). Drills should be 1 in. deep and 15 in. apart. In autumn or early winter, spinach beet supplies leaves that take the place of spinach in autumn or early winter. It is also known as "Perpetual Spinach" and some people prefer it. The drills should be 18 in. apart. You can sow it in April and again in July.

Seakale beet is also known as "Silver Beet" or "Swiss Chard." It is a dual-purpose vegetable. The leaf stems are large and white, but the leaf is green. You can cook the green part of the leaves as spinach and the white stalks and mid-ribs, stripped of foliage, may be cooked like seakale. You can sow this in

April, too—drills 1 in. deep and 18 in. apart. Later on, you thin the seedlings as you would with spinach or spinach beet. With the last two, you thin out to 3 in. apart in the first instance, removing alternate seedlings after about a fortnight. With seakale beet, the first thinning should be to 4 in. apart, finally leaving about 8 in. between plants.

TURNIPS

You can sow turnips in April. But if you are following the Ministry's cropping plan, you will wait until July, so we will deal with this crop in a later Guide.

ONIONS

Now is the time to plant out *onions* raised under glass. Harden the plants off gradually and plant them out in rows 1 ft. apart, leaving 6 in. between each plant. See that each bulb is set just on top of the ground and press the soil firmly around its roots.

A REMINDER ABOUT THE FRUIT GARDEN

In the March Guide we reminded you about spring dressings for your fruit trees and the spraying of your fruit bushes with lime sulphur. April is the time, so just turn to page 8 of the March issue and refresh your memory.

About those PESTS

Wartime gardeners, who may have suffered badly from the ravages of pests, may well have thought that gardening is just one long discouraging fight. But the "old hands" know that is not so ; they know, too, that by keeping their plots as clean as they can, and by taking early measures to cope with any marauders that may appear, they can do much to reduce their losses and keep the pests in check.

First, a few wise words about what you can do to prevent pest damage before you start to use insecticides. Strong plants are less likely to be destroyed—and you only get strong plants by good cultivation and manuring. You must not expect insecticides to make up for deficient cultivation and manuring. Another important step is to get rid of

the things that harbour pests : weeds, surplus seedbed plants, old brassica stumps and infested leaves. Growing the same crop on the same bed year after year also encourages pests, so that is another important reason for crop rotation. And then don't be finicky about hand-picking caterpillars when you do find them.

Some gardeners regard all creeping and flying things as foes. That is a mistake, for they include friends as well. Let us for a moment consider some of the insects you may find under and above ground. Of the "underground" enemies, there is first the wireworm : the commonest garden foe that particularly fancies potatoes, tomatoes and carrots. It is three-quarters of an inch long and has six legs. When you find it, break it in half or squash it.

5

Later on in life it turns into a "Click" beetle or "Skipjack"; it is called a "Click" because if you put in on its back it jumps to it with a click. If you suffer badly from wireworm, it is worth trying to trap them. On old potato makes a good trap, or three inches of old kale or Brussels stalk split down the middle. Put these traps a few inches below ground in spring, marking the spots with sticks. You can do a great deal to rid yourself of wireworm if you set traps regularly.

But don't mistake the centipede for a wireworm. You can tell the centipede by the number of its

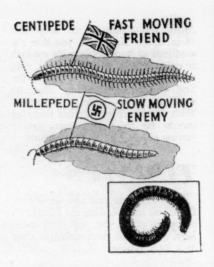

CENTIPEDE FAST MOVING FRIEND

MILLEPEDE SLOW MOVING ENEMY

WIREWORM TWICE ACTUAL SIZE

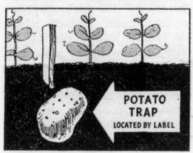

POTATO TRAP
LOCATED BY LABEL

legs—a pair to every section of its body. Don't kill the centipede, for it goes for your enemies—small slugs, worms and insects. The friendly centipede moves very quickly, while the millepede—a nasty sort of chap—moves slowly, though he has got two pairs of legs to every section, as against the centipede's one. You cannot go far wrong if you kill the slow-movers and let the fast movers live. Anyhow, it's death to the millepede that attacks the roots of most of your plants!

When you are getting the gound ready for planting in spring, look out for another enemy that works underground and attacks most crops—the leather jacket, the grub of the fly you call "Daddy Long Legs." One leather jacket can do much harm to many plants like lettuce and spinach, so you must kill him wherever you find him.

When the young plants begin to grow up, they meet new enemies —the chaps that do their work above ground. Most readers of

LEATHER JACKET

this Guide may have suffered from black fly, especially if they have grown broad beans. These black flies harm the plant by sucking the sap and injuring the tissues; if they are allowed to go on, they will spread from the shoot to the cluster of young bean pods and spoil the whole crop. Now the black fly's bitterest foe is the lady-bird, but although she makes all her meals off black or green flies, she cannot cope with all of them. The black fly usually attacks the top of the plant first, just when it is beginning to flower, so pinch off the top to check it. The lady-bird won't mind. But if the black fly spreads despite your efforts—and the lady-bird's

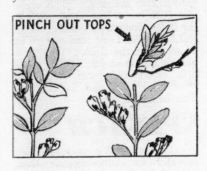

PINCH OUT TOPS

—act as advised at the end of this note, where hints are given for dealing also with slugs, caterpillars, flea beetles and the cabbage root fly. But first a word or two about these other pests that may come your way.

One of the dangers of leaving a lot of rubbish lying about the garden is that it harbours slugs that will attack your lettuce, so that is an argument in favour of a clean garden, with suitable rubbish put in its proper place—the compost heap—and unsuitable stuff burned.

SLUGS

Cabbage white butterflies are pests of the first order. It is bad enough to have to cope with our own native butterflies, but we also have to deal with the lot that fly over from the Continent every year. They come first in the spring and early summer, and leave us their eggs before they die. The eggs are laid on all kinds of cabbage crops, sometimes on stocks, nasturtiums and other plants. They are yellow, oval and pointed at one end. You will find the eggs in batches of 20 to 100 ; in about a fortnight they hatch out into young caterpillars that swarm together. You can tell them by their colour—bluish or greenish black, with a yellow line down the back and yellow sides. Their hairs are rather straggly. In about a month they are fed up—with your cabbages—and creep away to turn into chrysalides. About three weeks later, at the end of July or beginning of August, out come the butterflies which lay their eggs, and you get the second and more

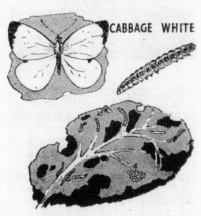

CABBAGE WHITE

dangerous lot of caterpillars that do harm in August and September.

The Cabbage White Butterfly has a pal—the small white butterfly that is responsible for the velvety green caterpillars. This butterfly lays her eggs one at a time and not in groups like the "Cabbage White." There is only one thing to do with any sort of caterpillar : pick them off and squash them. And squash any eggs you can find as well. It is a messy business, but it is worth it.

Another wretched pest is the cabbage aphis—the nasty greyish powder patches of insects that you may find on your plants. And then you may find holes in your young turnip leaves or in your young cabbages. They are the work of the flea beetle, which hops about so quickly that it is difficult to catch sight of. It eats the plant before it pops its head above the ground and keeps on with the foul work after the rough leaf appears.

Now here are the measures you are recommended to take for dealing with the most important pests that may come your way, though it is to be hoped they won't. And remember that early action may save you a lot of bother later on.

FLEA BEETLE

SLUG : Destroy with well-mixed "Meta" bait ; $\frac{1}{4}$ oz. with $\frac{3}{4}$ lb. slightly wet bran broadcast very thinly on soil—3 oz. per square rod—or dot small heaps over affected area.

CABBAGE CATERPILLAR

Dust plants at *first sign* of damage with Derris dust or spray with Derris insecticide. Repeat immediately more young caterpillars appear.

MUSLIN BAG

FLEA BEETLE

Dust seedlings with Derris, Nicotine or Naphthalene dust. Repeat two or three times at intervals of four days.

CABBAGE ROOT FLY

½ TEASPOONFUL CALOMEL DUST

Prevent attack by putting $\frac{1}{2}$ teaspoonful of 4 per cent. Calomel dust on soil around each plant as soon as set out. Repeat a fortnight later.

BLACK FLY, GREEN FLY, CABBAGE APHIS

Spray with Derris or Nicotine wash. If sunny and warm, dust with Nicotine Dust. Destroy all old cabbage stumps before mid-May.

Wt. T.24763/8564 100M 4/45 7/4 CN&CoLtd

UNWINS
OF HISTON

Autumn 1941

WAR TIME CATALOGUE
AND GARDEN GUIDE

OFFERING

Seeds of Quality

With

practical hints how to grow them

THE PRIME MINISTER
endorses the appeal of
THE MINISTER OF AGRICULTURE

"Every endeavour must be made . . . to
produce the greatest volume of food of
which this fertile island is capable—"

The Rt. Hon. WINSTON S. CHURCHILL

W. J. UNWIN LTD., Seedsmen, Histon, Cambridge

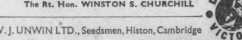

*Seed catalogues were available but, because of paper shortages, they
were not sent out to customers unless they wrote and asked for one.*

May

Victory in Europe was declared on 8th May 1945 and VE celebrations broke out all over England – except for on the allotment plot. Spring, let alone summer, was only just on the horizon for the gardener. As a whole the war years had been colder than normal, with the Januarys of 1940 and 1945 almost the coldest of the previous half century.

Little did the writers of the Guide know that worse was to come with the dreaded spring of 1947 when temperatures dropped in places to –21°C (-6°F) and root crops were frozen in the ground! Weather like this made gardeners wary of planting out tender tomato plants until the very end of May or even into June. This colder weather, combined with conservative eating habits, was also responsible for the lack of gardening enthusiasm for such crops as aubergines, grapes, sweetcorn or smooth skinned cucumbers, all of which are now commonly seen on allotment plots.

In a pre-plastic age poly-tunnels were unknown and shortages of fuel meant that glasshouses remained unheated for the duration of the war. Even in poor weather, the end of May saw the first potato plants appearing, Brussels sprouts and celery being planted out and runner beans being sown. The cultivation of runner beans posed a serious problem by 1945, as bamboos and other long stakes were in short supply, prompting a rush on seeds of dwarf bean varieties and even pilfering of bean poles.

MINISTRY OF — AGRICULTURE

ALLOTMENT &
Garden Guide

VOL. 1 No. 5   **MAY · 1945**

" Button to chin till May be in,
Cast not a clout till May be out "

And then some people say "Marry in May, repent alway". Perhaps if we do marry in May we may find the maid—like the month—fickle and fitful ; sometimes sunny, sometimes stormy—and sometimes more than a bit frosty ! That is the trouble with May, those killing frosts that do so much damage to our fruit blossom and young potato plants, and catch the unwise and unwary who put out their tomato plants too early and without protection. The end of May is quite soon enough for tomato planting. Too often we gardeners cling to tradition and get too far ahead with our sowing and planting, regardless of how our weather varies and how treacherous it can be.

However, May should be a busy month with all of us—so here's

hoping you will be "as full of spirit as the month of May". And watch out for those frosts !

May is a month for many jobs on the vegetable plot and it's not easy to keep pace with them all. Let's just list them now and deal with them in turn. Here they are :—

Thinning seedlings ; earthing up potatoes ; mulching peas and beans ; top dressing certain crops ; sowing winter greens in the seedbed and planting out Brussels ; making successional sowings of earlier crops ; sowing runners and marrows ; planting out tomatoes ; attending to the compost heap and keeping an eye open for pests.

Now let's say a bit about each of them.

Thin SEEDLINGS

Always try to seize the opportunity, if the ground's fairly moist and the weather cool with a promise

of warm showers to come, to thin any crops that need it—lettuce, spinach, parsnips and, later on, spring-sown onions. If these crops need thinning when the soil is too dry and the weather seems set fair, water them thoroughly before thinning and again as soon as you have finished. This will prevent too great a disturbance of the seedlings remaining while their neighbours were being pulled out.

Generally thin seedlings twice: first leaving twice as many plants as you will need; at the second thinning remove every other plant. Always pull out the weakest seedlings, leaving the strongest to grow on. Hoe between the rows, removing any seedling weeds at thinning time, and leaving the plot tidy.

Earth up POTATOES

It is important that during the period of active growth your potato plot should be hoed and kept free from weeds. If there is a danger of frost when the young plants appear, cover them lightly with soil. The first

up helps to keep the haulms upright, and prevents the tubers from being exposed to the light, which would make them go green. Incidentally, a good covering of soil over the tubers protects them in case of an outbreak of blight on the foliage. Blight spores don't work down the stems to the tubers,

earthing up should be done when the plants are some 6 in. high, and further soil should be drawn up to form a ridge about three weeks later. But don't cover up the leaves this time—they need all the light and air that they can get. Earthing

as some people think; they drop from the haulm directly on to the soil. So make your ridge as illustrated; don't leave a very pronounced furrow at the top, into which rain may wash the blight.

MULCH PEAS & BEANS

Both peas and beans specially need moisture to produce a good crop. In very dry weather, instead of watering, spread grass mowings, decayed leaves or compost to a depth of 1 in. along each side of the rows.

TOP DRESS. Very young plants, such as lettuce and spinach, will appreciate a top dressing of

sulphate of ammonia—about ½ oz. to the yard run.

Greens for the Seedbed

May is the month for sowing in the seedbed seeds of sprouting broccoli (mid-May), winter cabbage (also mid-May), kale and savoy (late May). How to use a seedbed was described in the March issue of this Guide (page 3).

Plant BRUSSELS SPROUTS

May to June is the period for planting out your Brussels. The Ministry's plan provides for two

TAKE CARE IN LIFTING FROM SEED BED

rows, 2½ ft. between rows and the same distance between plants. Don't forget that the plants need a long season of growth to develop properly. If your ground is poor, you would do well to fork well into the surface, before planting, 2 oz. to the square yard of some complete fertiliser such as "National Growmore", which is of special value to crops that have to stand the winter.

Be careful in lifting from the seedbed to see that you get a good ball of soil round the roots. Should the weather be dry, water the

seedbed row the night before. Plant with a dibber deep enough to bury the roots and stem up to the first leaves. Press the soil firmly round the plant with the dibber or your heel. If you plant in dry weather give the plants a good watering. Some gardeners practise puddling, placing soil and water in a bucket and plunging the plants' roots in it before planting. If the dry weather continues, water the plants each day, if you can, until they are established and show

signs of making new growth. Hoe frequently between rows and plants. To make watering more effective some gardeners plant in a drill about three or four in. deep.

SOW FOR SUCCESSION

Beet, carrots, lettuce and radishes (see March and April Guides for directions).

Sow RUNNERS

Runners do best on soil well trenched and given a good dressing of manure or compost, as advised in the February Guide (page 8). Clay soils are usually too wet and cold for them.

One pint will sow a double row of 50 ft. The plants are very tender and seeds should not be sown in

the open until May, though early crops may be secured by sowing in boxes in a frame or a greenhouse and transplanting later. In the open, sow the seed in double rows with 9 in. of space between the plants. For single rows, the plants should stand 12 in. apart.

If you have double rows, it is an advantage for staking to put the

3

plants opposite each other. It is a mistake to overcrowd runner beans. Seeds are best sown in a trench and should be placed 2 in. deep. Don't forget to sow a few extra at the end of the rows to fill up gaps in the rows.

Runner beans produce best when supported by stakes or some other contraption that allows them to climb ; they can also be grown as dwarf

plants by pinching out the growing shoots as they appear, but the yield will not be so heavy. Stout, straight

stakes 6-8 ft. long, without branches or twigs, are best for runner beans. Stakes are inserted against each plant and slightly inclined so that they cross at the top, allowing for a cross stake to be fixed as illustrated.

During dry weather, runner beans derive great benefit from watering ; in fact, drought is often responsible for the flowers dropping and failing to set. To induce a good set it may be

necessary to syringe the flowers with water. Keep the beans closely gathered as they mature, so as to prolong cropping.

Sow MARROWS

Choose a sunny corner for your marrows, digging in some well-rotted manure or compost into the bottom of the bed, which should be taken out one spit deep. Sow towards the end of May, placing groups of four or five seeds about 6 in. apart and 1 in. deep. Eventually thin to two plants, 12 to 15 in. apart.

Take care not to let the young plants suffer from lack of water ; give them plenty in dry weather and hoe regularly to keep the bed free from weeds.

Plant CELERY

If you want to grow celery (and you have not been able to sow seeds in heat), you should buy the plants ready for planting out in late May or June. Celery likes richly prepared ground. Dig out a trench 18 in. wide and 1 ft. deep, and fork in manure or compost into the bottom of it, returning the soil to within 3 in. of the level of the ground. Set the plants carefully in staggered double rows, 1 ft. apart—10 to 12 in. between plants. Water them in and give them plenty of water when the

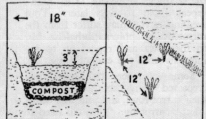

weather is dry. Dust with soot at intervals, as a prevention against leaf maggot. Earthing up will be dealt with in the June Guide.

Some people like *celeriac*—a turnip-rooted celery—for flavouring stews. You may like to try a row as an experiment. Plant in shallow drills 18 in. apart, 12 in. between plants. Celeriac also needs plenty of water in dry weather. Remove side shoots as they appear and hoe regularly.

The popular war-time crop..
TOMATOES

Judging by the response to the Ministry's advertisements in earlier years, the tomato is crop No. 1 with war-time gardeners and allotment holders. Unfortunately, despite many warnings, some amateurs have been taken in every year by unscrupulous people who sell them tomato plants far too early for planting outside. It is foolish to hope that the danger of frost is past until at least the end of May. As with so many gardening jobs there is no fixed date for planting ; it varies from about May 20 in the south-west to the end of the second week in June in the north. Little is gained and much may be lost by rushing plants out of doors a week or ten days before the weather has warmed up. The plants do not grow away well, and if the nights are cold they turn a dark, unhealthy colour and are seriously checked.

Always buy your plants from a reliable supplier. A well-grown tomato plant should be sturdy and short-jointed-about 6 or 8 in. high, with the buds of the first flower truss visible in the head of the plant. The distance between the leaves should be small and the leaves should be dark and of a bluish tinge. As a rule, plants produced in pots are best for planting in the open. Avoid "leggy" plants at all costs.

To grow tomatoes successfully

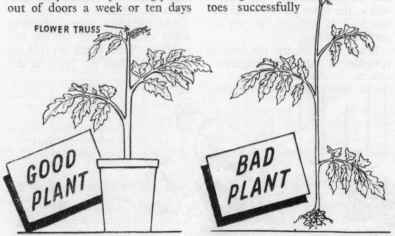

FLOWER TRUSS

GOOD PLANT

BAD PLANT

5

in the open you must have a good site. The best spot would be in the shelter of a wall or fence facing south or south-west, because there the temperature won't fall too low at night. The plants will get some sunshine there and be protected from the cold east winds we often get early in June. Get the ground ready well in advance of planting. Take out a trench 9 to 12 in. deep and 15 to 18 in. wide and dig in compost or well-rotted manure into

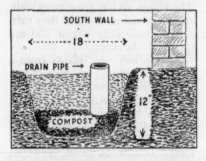

the second spit. For watering during summer get some unglazed drainpipes, if you can, and put them upright into the trench, 3 ft. apart. Then fill up the trench with the soil you took out. These pipes will let the water get to the subsoil, which it is difficult to wet by surface watering.

When you fill up the trench, sprinkle a suitable fertiliser—"National Growmore", for instance—over the surface : 1 to 2 oz. to every yard of trench, and mix it in with a fork.

The plants should be at least 18 in. apart in the row ; if you have more than one row, make the rows 3 ft. apart. Measure and mark out beforehand where the plants should go, putting in a 4 ft. stake at each position.

Before planting, make sure that the ball of soil round the roots is really wet. If you have bought plants in pots, stand them in water for about 20 minutes so that the ball is completely covered. Drain away excess water before planting.

Plant with a trowel. When planting from pots, take care not to damage the roots when you take the ball of soil out of the pot. Make the hole about $\frac{1}{2}$ in. to 1 in. deeper than the height of the ball of soil. Then put the ball in the hole and pack the soil tightly round it. Make a saucer-like depression round each plant : it is very useful for watering, and the absence of loose soil round the base of the stem makes it difficult for wireworm to get in.

Immediately after planting, water each plant to set the soil round it. Then watch out that the ball of soil does not begin to dry

out. If it does, give each plant about a pint of water.

When you have finished planting, tie the plants to the stakes you put in as markers. Tie loosely; a good guide is to leave room for your thumb to go between plant and stake. As the plant grows, tie it again to keep it upright, and remove every side shoot that appears in the corners formed by the leaf stalks and the main stem. These side shoots are usually dealt with when they are about 1 to $1\frac{1}{2}$ in. long. Don't let them get too big; if that happens, cut them off close to the stem with a sharp knife. More about tomatoes next month.

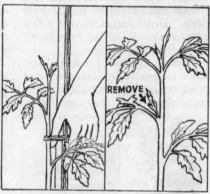

Attend to the Compost Heap

The importance of compost was described in the January Guide, and the March issue dealt with how to make it. May is the time of the year when further materials such as waste vegetable matter, coarse grass, lawn mowings and annual weeds, become available for the heap. While not forgetting the needs of domestic livestock, all the waste material that can be collected should be rotted down on the compost heap.

Look out for PESTS

If you are growing broad beans, look out for signs of black fly and tackle this pest early, as advised on page 6 of the April Guide. If you are growing early turnips, you may be troubled with the flea beetle. Last month's Guide also dealt with that.

To prevent the depredations of the onion fly, sprinkle 4% calomel dust along the rows of spring onions when the seedlings are about $1\frac{1}{2}$ in. high; repeat about 10 days later. Your seedling carrots may suffer from the carrot fly, so apply naphthalene dust to the rows and repeat at 10-day intervals until the end of June.

Some gardeners put lengths of creosoted string about 2 in. above their carrot rows, and find this wards off the carrot fly. You will need to dress the string with creosote three times (at fortnightly intervals, beginning mid-May) for early sowings and five times for the maincrop. You can put the creosote on with a brush or take the string up and re-dip it. You must not allow any of the liquid to splash on to the plants or it will "burn" the leaves.

A bit about BIRDS

The nesting season of wild birds is in full swing in May. Soon the birds themselves will reach their peak of usefulness to man. Robin, wren, hedge-sparrow, song-thrush and many others will be about their business of finding food for hungry nestlings, and so will be making constant inroads on garden pests.

ROBIN

True, the song-thrush may later take small toll of your bush fruit; but, all the same, this bird is the gardener's very good friend. Of all our birds, it is the champion snail killer; if it were no more than that, it would deserve protection and encouragement. As for robin, wren and hedge-sparrow—nobody has anything but good to say of them; in fact, there is nothing but good to say. Any or all of them may nest in gardens; if any of them nests in yours, let it nest in peace. Your interest and protection will be repaid a hundredfold.

TIT

THRUSH

Then there are the great tit and the blue tit. If you have a nest box in your garden—maybe even if you haven't—you may have the great good luck to harbour a family of either species. The last analysis of the food of these two feathered benefactors showed two-thirds injurious insects for the great tit, no less than three-quarters for the blue! What gardener would grudge such friends as these an occasional beakful of fruit?

It's a pity to add a discordant note; but there are birds you will need to watch. The house-sparrow, it is true, feeds its young on grubs and insects and takes a good many for itself; but it can be a nuisance when green things are coming through. If you are near a wood and there are jays about, look to your peas. If there are woodpigeons, look to anything in the garden that can be eaten.

HEDGE SPARROW

But apart from these few, the birds are your friends. If you give them a square deal, they will give you something better than that, for not all your labour or insect-icides will do so much to keep the garden clean. And, remember, the birds are on the job all day long.

BEWARE OF THESE!

HOUSE SPARROW   PIGEON   JAY

8

COOK WHAT
YOU GROW

6ᴰ
NET

by The
Shewell-Coopers

THE ENGLISH UNIVERSITIES PRESS LTD.

*Many publishers produced books and guides for the new gardeners,
showing them how to make the most of their home-grown food.*

June

Gardeners who had greeted the end of the war in Europe with relief, hoping for a return to rock gardens and roses, were in for a sorry surprise when the *Allotment & Garden Guide* for June arrived. True there was a picture of a rose bush on the front page (and a rare appearance of a woman!), but the accompanying text warned of a *'world food shortage which has now become a reality'*. Digging for Victory against Hitler was now redefined as Digging for Victory in the economic struggle for existence.

Exhortations to plan ahead, save seed and plant for the coming winter must have rung alarm bells for many. Alarm bells were also rung by the early appearance of signs of blight on potato plants. The traditional remedy for this, and one still widely used today and approved under organic regulations, was Bordeaux Mix. Nowadays this is readily available as a pre-prepared mix, but in the 1940s most gardeners still preferred to make their own. Consisting of copper sulphate, hydrated lime and water, this needed to be handled carefully and mixed only in an earthenware or enamelled jug. A correct mix had a distinctive blue colour, a colour which remains on the plants that are sprayed. To add to the blue of the Bordeaux, black soot was recommended for celery fly, and white Calomel dust for onion fly. June was a colourful time on the wartime allotment!

MINISTRY OF AGRICULTURE

ALLOTMENT &

Garden Guide

VOL. 1 No. 6   **JUNE - 1945**

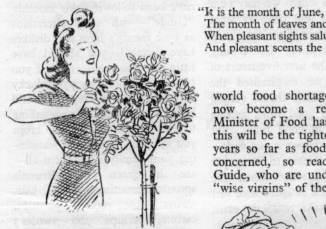

"It is the month of June,
The month of leaves and roses,
When pleasant sights salute the eyes,
And pleasant scents the noses."

world food shortage which has now become a reality. The Minister of Food has told us that this will be the tightest of the war years so far as food supplies are concerned, so readers of this Guide, who are undoubtedly the "wise virgins" of the parable, will

TO the poet "June rose by May dew impearled" may have been among the possible best things in the world ; but in these strictly utilitarian times we gardeners and allotment holders may feel that the sight of our vegetable plot coming along nicely with a variety of crops is not only a distinctly pleasant sight but a solid insurance premium against that threatened

be patting themselves on the back that they did not rest on their spades, but continued to "Dig for Victory"—not only victory in the fighting war, but victory in the economic struggle for existence that will be the aftermath of war.

Taking stock

June is the gardener's sort of halfway house—a time for taking stock and finding out where we stand. So after patting ourselves on the back, let's survey our plots, and assess our progress to date and the extent to which we may be a bit backward and consider what needs to be done if we are not to be caught napping this coming winter. In the first five issues of this Guide we emphasised the need for planning ahead, getting our needs in good time, getting things done in good time. But gardening on paper is too easy—and it's not so easy to put paper advice into practice when the weather or lack of spare time just puts paid to the best laid plans issued by a government department or the gardening papers.

What we gardeners have to bear in mind always is that lean period from about February until the end of May. Anyone can grow vegetables in summer—and get gluts of them ; but it is those winter vegetables that need more

thought and attention. If you have been following this monthly "Guide"—with such alterations as your family's likes and dislikes have dictated—you should have little cause to worry ; but if you have so far been happy-go-lucky in your choice of crops, you still have time in June to do something to put matters right. The crops you want for next winter—assuming your family likes them all—are the green crops—Brussels sprouts, sprouting broccoli, kale, savoys ; the roots — parsnips, carrots, turnips and swedes ; onions and leeks ; dried peas and beans ; potatoes.

It is too late to do anything about potatoes, onions and parsnips, if they are not already growing on your plot. While it is too late to sow seeds of Brussels sprouts, sprouting broccoli, kale and savoys, you can order some

Crops for the lean period

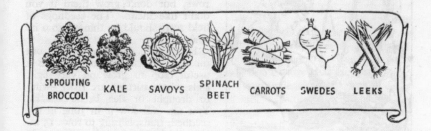

SPROUTING BROCCOLI   KALE   SAVOYS   SPINACH BEET   CARROTS   SWEDES   LEEKS

plants of the last three from your usual nursery or shop. Kale and sprouting broccoli should be put out about mid-July, savoys later in that month or in early August. Though it is rather late to plant Brussels, there is just the chance that you may get a fair crop if you put in the plants at once.

During July, too, you could sow a row of spinach beet that, given favourable conditions, should give you a crop of excellent green leaves next winter and right on through the spring.

If you like leeks and have not sown seeds in the seedbed, you can get some plants and put them out in July.

As to root crops, main crop carrots can be sown in June to early July, swedes at the end of June, turnips in July.

The experts tell us that we need some of that precious body-building stuff—protein—in our diet. Now dried peas and beans are a valuable source of protein, and it is worth while saving some of our crops for the purpose, as well as to provide seeds for sowing next year—always assuming that we save our own seeds, a subject which will be dealt with in a later Guide. Do your saving systematically, however. Don't just leave a few late pods on each plant, but reserve a number of plants at each end of the row.

Having looked ahead and made sure—at least in our minds—that we are not going to be caught napping in the few months from next February, let us come back to the present for a bit and concentrate on essential jobs of the month. First, *thinning*—and no apology is made for returning once more to this important operation. And don't forget to keep that hoe going regularly.

3

THINNING

This needs to be done now practically every week. Beet, carrots, parsnips, lettuce and spinach have all to be thinned as they become large enough. Thinning was dealt with in the May "Guide" and all that it is necessary to add now is that it is a good time to apply a little fertilizer after the plants have been thinned and are beginning to grow strongly. A dressing of ½ oz. of sulphate of ammonia can be hoed in per yard of row.

TOMATOES

The May "Guide" dealt with the planting of tomatoes. To get the best results keep each plant to the main stem, pinching out the side-shoots that come in the corners formed by the leaf stalks and the main stem. Keep the plants *well watered* and feed them regularly with a good complete fertilizer. There are a number of proprietary brands of tomato fertilizer that should be used according to the suppliers' instruc-

tions. Or you can use "National Growmore." A good working rule is to apply a teaspoonful per plant as each truss of fruit sets.

When watering, remember that it is useless just to damp the soil surface, for this merely encourages surface rooting. You must water well, giving about half-a-gallon to each plant. Tomato fruits are often split when the plants are given a heavy watering after having been dry. That is because the skin gets hard and inelastic and cannot expand when the fruit swells after a good watering, so it splits or cracks. So don't let the plants get dry.

PINCH OUT

FRUIT TRUSS

1 TEASPOONFUL FERTILISER PER PLANT AS EACH TRUSS SETS.

"Blight" is the chief disease likely to affect tomatoes in the open. It may attack only the fruit, but the stem and leaves may be affected as well. Intense brown or black blotches are the signs, and infected fruits often fall off the plant. The discoloured areas are edged with a downy white growth. It's the same blight that attacks potatoes. To control it, spray your plants with a copper spray (see next section).

Take care of your POTATOES

Potatoes are growing strongly now. In most places they have been earthed up. Remember, when earthing, not to draw the soil up to a greater height than about 6 in. and do not leave a flat top or trough to the ridge. Finish it off to as sharp a point as possible. This prevents spores of potato blight from being washed down by rain to infect the tubers. Don't try to earth up when the soil is wet.

To a large extent the danger of blight attack depends on the weather : if dry, only local attacks are likely and will not cause serious damage ; given frequent spells of warm, moist weather, the tops may be completely killed by the end of July or in August. The effect on the crop would be serious, if the tops were badly affected. The weight of crop would be greatly reduced ; and if the disease spreads to the tubers themselves, they may rot in the ground or after you have stored them.

WHAT TO DO. If you live within 10 or 12 miles of a large industrial centre, where the air is laden with fumes and smoke, do not spray, but seek advice locally : the secretary of your local allotment society, the horticultural committee of the council or the park superintendent should be able to help you. Gardeners who are not in areas likely to be affected by fumes from factories should, as a form of insurance against blight, spray their potato foliage with one of the copper-containing sprays recommended for the purpose. Perhaps the simplest course is to buy one of the ready-made Bordeaux powders or pastes and apply it according to the maker's instructions. Usually you have only to mix it with water and it is less trouble to prepare than a home-made mixture.

If you have a hand-dusting machine, you could apply one of the powders made for the purpose —copper-lime or Bordeaux dust. Dust needs to be applied more often than sprays, however—four or five applications should be given, allowing a fortnight each.

WHEN TO SPRAY. The right time for the first dusting or spray-

ing is just before the leaves of the potatoes meet in the rows ; this

5

usually happens at the end of June or early in July. Don't wait until you see blight spots on the leaves—if you do find any, spray at once. If dusts are used, further applications are needed every fortnight ; with the spray, a second application after three weeks should be sufficient. But if the blight attack is severe, a third spraying may be needed in August.

Making Bordeaux Mixture

If you prefer to make your own Bordeaux mixture here is the recipe. The quantities mentioned will make enough spray for about 2 rods of potatoes. Put 2½ gallons of water into a bucket ; pour off a quart of the water into an *earthenware* or *enamelled* jug, and dissolve 4 oz. of copper sulphate in it (powdered or granular copper sulphate is preferable, as it dissolves easily). In the bucket containing the remaining water dissolve 5 oz. of *fresh* hydrated lime and stir well. When the copper sulphate has all dissolved, pour the blue solution slowly into the bucket containing the lime solution, stirring all the time. It is then ready for use and should be used the day it is made. To avoid clogging your sprayer, it is worth while straining the solution through a piece of muslin. Immediately after use always rinse the bucket or other container, as well as the sprayer, with clean water in which a little washing soda has been dissolved.

Points to Remember

You can use a stirrup pump, if you obtain a fine spray nozzle for it.

A misty spray is best, as it wets the foliage easily.

If you have no sprayer, you can use a watering can with a fine rose.

Make certain that *both* sides of the foliage as well as the stems are thoroughly wetted.

Choose a fine day so that the spray has time to dry before the next fall of rain.

It is much easier if you can co-operate with some friends or neighbours and spray several batches of potatoes on the same day.

Earthing up CELERY

Before you earth-up, tie the celery plants loosely just below the leaflets and remove any side growths. When the plants are about 15 in. high, earth-up slightly, but see that the ground is thoroughly moist before

you begin. The second and third earthings—at three-weekly intervals—can be more thorough, until finally the soil should cover the plants right up to the leaves and should slope away neatly. Don't let any soil fall into the heart of the plant.

TIE LOOSELY

REMOVE SIDE GROWTHS

6

Are you watching out for those Pests?

Any signs of *black fly* yet? Some gardeners think that this pest is encouraged by broad beans, but there is no foundation for this. You may quite likely find it on your "runners." Wherever you come across it, take the measures recommended on pages 7 and 8 of the April Guide. And if you are growing broad beans, remove the growing tips when the plants are in full flower. If the winds are high and the plants look like being broken, put in a few stout stakes and run some stout string around the rows.

While the April Guide deals with other garden pests that may be a nuisance in June (slugs on your lettuce, cabbage root fly and carrot fly), it may not cover some pests that may trouble you. *Celery fly* for instance. Brown blisters may appear on the leaves. Watch the seedlings carefully for blistered leaves, and destroy them or crush them with your fingers. Dust the plants weekly with soot to prevent egg laying. If the attack is serious, spray the leaves (both sides) with a nicotine and soap wash.

Then *onion fly* may also cause trouble, especially on dry soils. As a precaution dust the soil along each side of the rows with 4 per cent. Calomel when the plants are about an inch high.

Feed your CROPS

Beet, carrots, parsnips and onions benefit by a dressing of sulphate of ammonia after thinning—½ oz. to the yard run. If your carrots and onions are attacked by the fly, a similar dressing will help them considerably.

LETTUCE

Don't forget to sow a short row of seed every fortnight to ensure a succession. And if you transplant the thinnings from earlier rows, see that you give them a good start. Don't put them on lumpy ground and don't water them late on a cold evening or leave them without water at all. If the plot reserved for lettuce is lumpy and not easy to break down to a fine tilth, sift some fine soil over the surface, see that the seedlings are firmly planted and watered well at the right time until they are firmly established.

MARROWS

Although marrows are usually sown in the open towards the end of May, it's not too late to sow in June. In a sunny corner dig in some well-rotted manure or compost and set a few groups of seed—four or five seeds to each group—about 6 in. apart and 1 in. deep. Later, thin each group to two plants, 12 to 15 in. apart. Marrows need a lot of water. Make sure they get it, particularly in dry weather.

Couple of Tips

First, as to cabbages: when you cut one, make two nicks crosswise on the top of the stump, and within a month or six weeks it will sprout again and give you a crop of tender greens.

Second, if you have any grass left in your garden and are not using the mowings to feed stock or make compost, give your runner beans a mulch of 2 or 3 inches. This will

help to conserve the moisture and benefit the beans considerably.

More Root Crops

The main root crops may be sown in June or early July—beet (early June), maincrop carrots (June or early July) and swedes (mid-June). The sowing of beet and carrots was dealt with in the April Guide (p. 3), so the details will not be repeated here.

Bear in mind, too, that the above times for sowing are merely general reminders, and that gardeners must have regard to local conditions and advice from the experienced. For instance, as to carrots, in the midlands and the north, mid-June is regarded as the latest date to sow with an assurance of a good crop; while in the south and west, sowings may often be made with safety up to mid-July. Another point is that late-sown carrots are less liable to attacks by the "fly" than those sown earlier in the year.

SWEDES

Swedes are a safer crop in some districts than turnips. They can stand the cold better and can be left in the ground until after Christmas. Though there are garden varieties of swedes, the field sorts such as "Best of All" and "Eclipse" are really the best to grow.

Swedes are usually sown in mid-

June (earlier in the north) in drills 15 in. apart and 1 in. deep. The Ministry's plan provides for two rows, but don't grow them if you don't like them. The seedlings of field sorts should be thinned to 9 in. apart.

For those who like to try out unusual vegetables, *Kohl Rabi* is a useful crop to grow on very light soils where turnips are risky owing to drought or flea beetle attacks. You can still sow it in June in the seedbed, transplanting to rows 15 in. apart with 8 in. between plants. It is better, however, to drill in the ordinary way, like swedes and turnips, and thin out. *Kohl Rabi* should not be stored for any length of time, but should be eaten soon after lifting.

A word about Gathering Crops

Before the full spate of summer vegetables begins, a few words about gathering crops may not be out of place. Gather in the morning or evening, when they are fresh and not limp from the sun; handle them carefully, so that they come into the kitchen fresh and tempting. More important, however, is to gather crops before they are past their prime. It is a mistake to leave batches of cabbages, lettuces, peas and other vegetables until the whole crop is ready for use. So often the gardener cannot bring himself to gather his vegetables before they are fully matured, with the result that when they are ready, he is unable to cope with them all at once and many go to waste. Use your vegetables on the young side; they are more tasty, and the scientists tell us they do you more good than when they are old and tending to be tough. On the other hand, of course, don't be extravagant about it. There is no sense in picking them so young that a whole crop is used up in a meal or two.

Everyone was shown to be doing their bit in the garden, including royalty. Here Princess Elizabeth spreads a net over the strawberry patch she is cultivating.

July

July was to be the 'make or break' month: in the words of the 'Guide', *'What you do – or fail to do – this month, will determine how well or badly off your family will be for greens in the lean period from next February onwards'*. There was to be no post-VE Day slacking! Winter greens such as spinach beet, Brussels and spring cabbages were still the watchword. The 'play safe' gardener was advised to carry on following the Ministry's Cropping Plan, issued at the outbreak of war as Growmore Bulletin No. 1, and going strong ever since through all its Dig for Victory guises. The Guide had never bothered reproducing the plan itself as literally millions of copies had been made available in the previous five years.

Watering, one of the main tasks for the gardener in a good summer, could only be recommended cautiously in the Guide. The comment on page 2 *'assuming the water-supply situation is reasonably good'* did not herald rationing of water (surely the final straw!) but instead referred to the wide variation in facilities for water on different allotment sites. Sites in existence before the war, or set up with the support of large suburban councils, might have standpipes or troughs, but smaller sites in rural or urban areas, or in private parks or country house grounds, might not have any access to water. The weather during the war years had not often been hot and dry enough to necessitate sustained periods of watering. The summer of 1945 was, in fact, marked by too much rain.

MINISTRY OF AGRICULTURE

ALLOTMENT &

Garden Guide

VOL. 1 No. 7　　　　　　　　　　**JULY - 1945**

"The summer looks out from her brazen tower,
Through the flashing bars of July."

Well, given
that kind of July
weather—though
with our climate
we can never be
sure—we shall
feel like taking
a snooze in the deck chair or lying
down under a tree, instead of
getting on with those gardening
jobs that must be done. But we
must not make the mistake of
thinking that this month the
garden can be left to take care of
itself. For the weeds grow as well
as the vegetables, and pests and
diseases can quickly spread, if not
checked at the start. So even if
you feel like "just
a little sleep, a
little slumber, a
little folding of
the hands to
sleep," don't
indulge that
feeling too often,
and do keep that
hoe going, to

check the weeds.
*And watch out
for those pests.*

For instance,
the *"Cabbage
White"* butterfly
is now on the
wing; too soon its caterpillars
may be gorging on your green-
stuff. Your first method of
attacking these garden enemies
is to destroy the colonies of eggs
by crushing them between thumb
and forefinger. It's not a pleasant
job but it must be done. Then, if
the caterpillars do appear, destroy
them by hand-picking, or dust or
spray with derris (see April Guide).
Some people
complain that
they have tried
derris dust with
little or no effect.
Well, either the
dust was too old
and had lost its
killing property,
or only one

dusting was given. As successive broods of caterpillars hatch out, further dustings are necessary; fresh derris applied *as soon as caterpillars are seen* will help to control them. A dusting machine is a great convenience and the dust should be applied when there is dew on the leaves. Always try to get the dust right into the centre of the plants.

It is infuriating to go out one evening and find your cabbage plants suddenly wilting one by one. On digging up one of them you will probably find white grubs feeding on the roots. They are the grubs of the *cabbage root fly;* once the plant is attacked the only thing to do is to dig it out and burn it. The right thing to do is to apply a ring ($\frac{1}{2}$ teaspoonful) of 4 per cent. Calomel dust round each young plant of the cabbage family as you plant it out. This will put paid to the trouble.

The *Turnip Flea Beetle* may also be on the warpath, eating holes in your cabbage and turnip plants. It has caused gardeners trouble for centuries and is most troublesome during dry weather. Some old hands believe in the cold water cure, and give the plants a good soaking every night until they are about 6 in. high. But that's not possible on some allotments, so derris, nicotine or napthalene dust should be used, as recommended in the April Guide. And dust often till the leaves are well formed.

And don't forget that what you do—or fail to do—this month, will determine how well or badly off your family will be for winter greens in the lean period from next February onwards (see page 6).

Now having made up our minds to keep going at the job, let's have a look at some of the things we might do about our growing crops, before we get on to further sowings and plantings.

DIG UP & BURN AFFECTED PLANTS

DESTROY GRUBS

THE SAFEGUARD

½ TEASPOONFUL 4% CALOMEL DUST

Crops that need water

We shall probably need to be economical again this summer. It is difficult to lay down hard and fast rules about watering vegetables, and the gardener must use his own judgment. Newly transplanted seedlings may suffer seriously if water is withheld. But established plants may suffer if watered only at irregular intervals. Once you start watering you must carry on, so if the plants are holding their own in a dry spell, it is unwise to begin widespread watering unless you can do it regularly.

Assuming the water supply situation is reasonably good, crops that specially benefit by watering are runner beans, celery, marrows (specially on mounds) and tomatoes.

Planting out LEEKS

You can plant leeks from mid-June to mid-August, but July is the time recommended in the Ministry's cropping plan. Many gardeners plant them on ground cleared of peas. If you have sown leeks in your seedbed, the seedlings should be lifted when about 6 in. high. If the soil is dry, soak the seedbed before lifting. Lift carefully with a fork ; it is usual to cut off the tips of the leaves before planting out. Plant in rows 12 to 18 in. apart, 9 in. between plants. Drop each plant into a hole at least 6 in. deep, made with a blunt dibber. Water in to wash soil round the roots, but don't fill the hole with soil. The sketches show how to plant. Although hardy, the soil should be drawn up to crops in the autumn to give some protection from severe frost and to help in bleaching.

Feed your ONIONS

Early July is the best time to provide some extra rations for onions that have not had the advantage of heavy manuring before sowing or planting. A good general fertiliser such as "National Growmore" is safe and effective. The ideal time to apply any fertiliser is during showery weather ; and if showers are lacking, do not fail to hoe in the fertiliser and water thoroughly. Artificial manures of all sorts are more of a danger than a help when spread on dry ground, but their action is very soon seen when rain descends or when artificial watering has been well done. Not more than two applications of any fertiliser should be given to the onion bed. The ideal to aim at is hard, well-ripened bulbs—not mere size, for the medium bulbs will keep better than the big ones. Late manuring with artificials only prolongs the growing period and makes ripening all the later and more difficult, so give no artificials after mid-July.

Earthing up BRUSSELS

Draw a little soil up round the stems about a week after planting. Remember, Brussels sprouts like very firm ground.

3

Getting 'RUNNERS' to set

Syringe the plants, and particularly the flowers, with water during hot weather to encourage the beans to form. And pinch out the growing tips of the main shoots when the plants have reached the tops of the sticks.

Harvesting SHALLOTS

Shallots are ready for harvesting when the foliage has begun to wither. You then lift the little bunches of bulbs and leave them on the surface to dry off. But if the ground is heavy and moist, lay them out along a dry surface, such as a path, for a few days, for they must be well ripened and perfectly dry before storing. Or if you have got a strip of wire netting, you could dry them on this, raising it slightly from the ground to let a current of air pass beneath them. Then tie them into bundles or lay them in trays or boxes, and store in a dry, frost-proof, airy shed. Look them over from time to time and throw out any decaying bulbs.

STORED IN BUNDLES OR TRAYS

Try a row of SPINACH BEET

If you have not sown a row of spinach beet or seakale beet earlier, try a row now. Either is a valuable vegetable and often survives the winter better than any other green crop. Sow the seeds in drills about 1 in. deep and allow 8 in. between plants. Always use spinach beet when the leaves are young and tender.

Sow those TURNIPS

If you are following the Ministry's cropping plan, now is the time to sow turnips for storing on ground cleared of early potatoes, which should be in good condition for roots, as it will have been well worked during the past month or two. The rows should be 1 ft. apart and the seed sown about 1 in. deep.

Sow for succession

Sow lettuce every 10 or 14 days. And while you are about it, don't forget to make another sowing of *parsley*, for the experts tell us we don't eat nearly enough for our health's sake. Drills should be ½ in. deep.

Sowing SPRING CABBAGE

Of all early vegetables we look forward with most pleasure, perhaps, to our first cutting of spring cabbage. There is a delicacy, texture and flavour about it that no cabbage can aspire to at any other period of the year. At the end of the month sow the seeds.

Instead of sowing in a drill, try for once sowing broadcast on a small plot. Some people think you get far better plants that way. The seeds are sometimes sown far too thickly in drills and very poor plants result.

Don't waste that SUMMER WASTE

At this time of year garden "waste" is generally fairly plentiful and should not be wasted. Pea stems, potato haulms, outside lettuce leaves, the last of the rough leaves from spring cabbage, grass cuttings and the like should be made into compost, which, later on, you will dig back into your soil to maintain its fertility. How to make a compost heap was described in the March Guide.

There are some people who seem to think that the compost heap is a new idea, introduced because farmyard manure is hard to come by. It is no novelty, for the gardening books of a century or more ago mentioned it ; long before it was called "compost" the value of decayed vegetable refuse was well known and understood, particularly by the professional gardener.

CARROTS

If you would like to experiment with carrots, try sowing the seed broadcast in a broad flat drill 1 in. deep, instead of in the usual narrow drill. Late-sown carrots usually escape the attention of the carrot fly.

5

Those GREEN CROPS for next winter

During the summer, when the weather does not always provide those rainy periods at the time we need them most, we gardeners have to be swift to act and seize the right moment to do our various jobs of sowing and planting. When a fall of rain has brought the surface soil into just the right state for planting, all other garden work should be set aside to make the most of an opportunity that may not come again until the seedling plants have passed the best stage for planting out. If nature fails to oblige, then we have to choose between waiting for rain and risking the plants remaining in the seed-beds, or watering the ground thoroughly before planting. With kale and sprouting broccoli, two very useful vegetables for after Christmas, this is a decision we often have to make. The middle of the month is the time to plant them, in rows 2 ft. apart each way; if there is sufficient room, allow 2 ft. 6 in. each way. The Ministry's plan for a 300 sq. yd. plot recommends two rows of each, which should provide a good supply of green-stuff lasting well into next spring.

These brassicas should be planted in a shallow drill about 2 in. deep and 3 or 4 in. wide. This not only helps to direct moisture towards the roots of the plants, but it makes it easier to draw soil up to the stems, thus helping to keep the plants from blowing over on gusty days later in the season.

The Ministry's plan also provides for three rows of *winter cabbages*, and mid-July is the time for planting them out (2 ft. apart each way) in the shallow drills already described. If you have grown your own plants in a seed-bed, lift them carefully with a

TEST FOR FIRMNESS

fork, aiming at getting them out with as much soil as possible adhering to the roots. Should the weather be dry, give the seed-bed a good soaking the night before you lift. This applies to all your brassicas.

The sketches on planting cabbage may help you. If you have to plant in dry ground, water each hole before planting, cover in with soil and again water. Half-a-pint of water should be sufficient for each plant.

Always make sure that your cabbage plants are firmly planted by testing one or two here and there as you go along the rows.

If you pull the plant by the edge of a leaf, the part between your finger and thumb should tear away. But if you pull the plant up, you are not planting firmly enough.

Early-sown *savoys* will be reaching the stage when they should be transplanted. But it is not wise to have this crop in bearing too early in the winter, and if the larger plants are put out 2 ft. apart this month, the smaller seedlings could be transplanted 6 in. apart in an odd corner and allowed to grow on for a time before you finally put them in their permanent quarters, perhaps as late as the end of July or early in August.

On saving your own SEED

Some gardeners like having a shot at something new — seed saving, for example. Those who have not hitherto experimented in this direction might like to try it out. But it is well that they should know that while a few kinds of vegetable seeds can safely be saved by the amateur, others are best left to the experts.

You know that all flowering plants need pollen to fertilise the female part of the plant, so that it can produce seed. Some plants are fertilised by their own pollen, while others have to get it from another plant. Broadly, those that fertilise themselves are "safe"; those that need pollen from another plant should be left to the professional seed grower. Why? Well, you may be growing, say, a cabbage for seed in your garden, while another gardener not far away may be growing a Brussels sprout plant for seed. The wind or the bees may bring pollen from your neighbour's plant to your own—and your plants next year

would be an unbelievable mixture, yet would be useless to you. Now, if that were to happen in your garden, how much more serious would it be if you were to allow one of your cabbages to flower and produce seed near a commercial grower's field of Brussels sprouts growing for seed. It might cause immense trouble and ruin the quality of his seed. The only "safe" vegetables for seed-saving purposes are peas, beans of all kinds, onions, leeks, tomatoes, lettuce, ridge cucumbers and marrows.

Now is the time to mark the plants you intend to save. The best and easiest way is to tie a label on part of your rows of peas and beans and leave *all* the pods on the plants in that section for seed. Don't pick any at all for the kitchen. So often gardeners leave the last few pods on their plants. These are usually small, weakly pods and do not give really good seed. If you remember that one-tenth of your pea and bean crop

7

should give you sufficient seed to sow a similar area again next year, you will be able to judge how many plants to leave. Most allotment

rows are 30 ft. long, so of your peas you would need to have 3 ft. at one end of the row. Runner beans are usually a little more prolific, so one-twentieth of each row is usually enough to save for next year's sowing.

One good lettuce plant should give you all the seed you will need. Mark and label the best plant you have. Don't choose one that has "bolted" or run to seed instead of making a good large heart. It may produce offspring that will do the same thing next year and then you would get very few lettuces worth cutting. If the heart is very hard and firm, make a cut with a knife in the shape of a cross on the heart. Don't cut too deeply, but just through the first three or four layers of leaves. This will make it easy for the flower head to push its way up. That is all you need to do for the present.

If you spring planted any of last season's onions and left leeks in the ground for seed, they will be coming into flower now. See that the stems, which are very brittle, are tied securely to stakes, but

otherwise there is nothing to do to them until the end of September, for onions, and/or mid-October, for leeks. A later Guide will tell you how to harvest the seed.

When your marrows are bearing fruits, pick out one good-sized fruit and scratch the word "seed" on it with a pencil. When your tomatoes are carrying good trusses of fruits, pick out a good, shapely truss, mark it with a piece of raffia and watch this Guide for further advice.

The plants that you have selected for seed saving should be

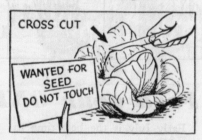

inspected carefully to see that they do not develop disease in any way. Leave the pods or fruits to ripen as long as possible. But with lettuces, as soon as you see little tufts of fluff forming on the seed heads, pick them and put them in a shallow cardboard box or a seed-box with a sheet of paper on the bottom. You may have to look at your lettuce plant every day when it is nearing the ripening stage, as a sudden heavy downpour of rain may wash all the seeds on to the ground, if they have reached the fluffy stage. In rainy periods it is best to pull the lettuce plant up, when nearing the harvest stage ; put it in a newspaper and finish the ripening in a warm room.

8

Wt. T4397/8638 125M 6/45 CN&CoLtd.

Printed for H.M. Stationery Office by Stafford & Co., Ltd., Netherfield, Nottingham. 51—5698. 2860/03

Potatoes were encouraged as an alternative food to bread
after initial difficulties with seed potato were overcome.

August

Weeds, wasps and brown rot awaited the diligent *Allotment & Garden Guide* reader in August. Few people nowadays would recognise all the weeds in the traditional rhyme 'Kex, charlock, thistle, spurry, pimpernel, quitch'. However, all are still common inhabitants of the allotment plot. Kex or kecksy meant weeds generally, charlock is a variety of wild mustard, spurry is a weed of corn and arable with small white flowers, scarlet pimpernel is now more commonly known as salad burnet, while quitch is couch grass.

Alongside the traditional rhyme, a popular wartime slogan crept into August's Guide, '*What feeds a weed will feed a cabbage to feed you*'. Wartime phraseology was everywhere: patriotic gardeners had to be wary of wasps arriving in 'battalions', and brown rot spores staged 'invasions' of the native orchard.

Storing gluts of summer produce was a vital element in the days before freezers and August's Garden Guide included reminders to salt runner beans, and pick apples for store before wasps could damage them. Soft fruits were 'stored' by making them into jams and preserves, although sugar rationing had restricted the amount that could be made. In fact many housewives might have objected to the use of a whole spoonful of jam in the wasp trap pictured on page 7! Apples ready for eating in August included the traditional 'Beauty of Bath', 'Irish Peach' and 'Gladstone', varieties now rarely found in shops and supermarkets as they lose flavour if stored.

M I N I S T R Y   O F   AGRICULTURE

ALLOTMENT &

Garden Guide

VOL. 1 No. 8   **AUGUST - 1945**

'This is the month of weeds
Kex, charlock, thistle . . .
Spurry, pimpernel, quitch . . .
Making for trouble.
This is the month of weeds.'

Before Roman holidays were popularised in these islands August was Weodmonath—the month of weeds. Nature probably realised that harvest would fully occupy man's attention at this time of the year, and cunningly contrived for most of the wickedest weeds to shed their seeds. The Romans just helped things along by encouraging everyone who was not helping with the harvest, to sit in the sun—to take a holiday. And very pleasant too—when these islands held but a handful of people, but holidays are not for the gardeners in a population of 48 million people on an island in a world short of food and short of ships to carry it. So—first of all—keep the hoe going. What feeds a weed will feed a cabbage to feed you.

Even if there were no weeds there would still be plenty to do in the garden, for this is the time of gathering the fruits of labour. And careful harvesting is just as important as careful sowing and careful growing.

Dwarf, French and runner beans require frequent picking or they will grow tough and stringy. If you have more than you and your friends can eat now, remember that they can be easily salted down for winter use. Regular picking of runner beans helps to make a longer fruiting season. But do not pick any beans from the plants you may have selected for seed.

Pull and use early beet. If left in the ground too long the roots will become woody and stringy. Any early-sown carrots that remain should be used up quickly. Summer turnips are ready to use, and marrows and tomatoes should be gathered as they ripen. Onions are important enough to have a section to themselves (see page 4).

Pick herbs now—just before they flower. Gather shoots of thyme, sage, mint, marjoram, tarragon and parsley. Tie them in bundles, wash them, cover with muslin to keep out dust and hang to dry in an airy shed or near the fire. When thoroughly dry and crisp, crush to a mealy texture and store in lidded jars or bottles away from the light.

Your last chance TAKE STOCK

Now is the time to make sure of winter's greenstuff—to make good losses caused by pests or diseases—to check your planning. Now is your opportunity to sit down after that back-aching weeding—just sit and think—sit and make sure—it's your last chance.

If you have not yet sown spring cabbage, do so at once or it will soon be too late. Do not sow in that part of the seedbed where spring sowings of cabbage were made this year. The soil may contain Cabbage Root Fly or the spores of Club Root. Sow seed thinly 1 in. deep in drills made 6 in. apart ; sow enough to plant four rows of spring cabbage on the ground which will be left free after the onions are harvested. Do not

sow too many, but allow a small reserve for making good any losses after planting out in September. If possible, sow after rain; or if the soil is very dry, water the seedbed a few hours before sowing. Where space is confined, sow "Harbinger", which is compact and hearty. Where more room is available "Early Offenham" and "Durham Early" are good varieties.

Sow late kale now where it is to mature, and thin as required during growth—it will give you a late green crop in March and April. Sow winter radish—they can be lifted and stored. Smooth-leaved Batavian endive, sown now and treated as lettuce, will last well into the winter, if it is blanched by tying up loosely with raffia and protected by a pot or box.

The main thing is to make sure of winter greens. Sow *now* for the lean months. If you are following the Ministry's Cropping Plan, make yourself completely comfortable in a deck chair—and study it. If you have any gaps or corners to spare, fill them with winter greens.

Prepare for AUTUMN SOWINGS

Ground for winter lettuce and turnips should be prepared a week or two in advance. Avoid ground likely to become damp in the winter ; lettuces can stand up to cold much better than to wet conditions.

Dig the ground over one spade's depth and leave it for a week or more to settle. If the soil is poor, rake in a dressing of 1-1½ oz. per square yard of National Growmore fertiliser. If the ground was not limed in the spring, dress with lime

and fork in lightly immediately after digging, but do not apply at the same time as the fertiliser. Leave the ground alone until the lime is well washed in and then—just before sowing—apply the fertiliser and fork it in lightly.

For lettuce, tread the ground firmly and evenly and rake it down finely. Choose a variety suitable for winter and sow seed thinly in drills ¼ in. deep and 1 ft. apart. When seedlings are large enough to be handled in late September and early October, they will be thinned out to 9 in. apart.

TOMATOES

Strong growth and plentiful flowers can be misleading. It is rare for us even in the best of summers to have the long spells of sunshine necessary to ripen more than four trusses of fruit. So "stop" the plants by pinching out the main growing shoot. Nip it off just above the fourth truss. Even if four trusses have not set, the stopping should be done by the third week of the month. There is nothing to be gained by leaving the plants to grow on.

Keep moisture at the roots. Allowing the soil to dry out and then trying to correct matters by soaking, only leads to split fruit. If you have the material, apply a generous mulch (see page 4) and do not let the soil surface cake hard. Keep feeding the plants, but do not overdo it; and especially at this stage avoid too much nitrogen— sulphate of ammonia or nitrate of soda—which will only promote rank growth and fruit that lacks flavour.

PINCH OUT HERE

It also makes the plants less resistant to disease.

Let the sun get at the fruit. This does not mean recklessly cutting out every leaf that is in the way. Remember that the leaves of plants play an important part in their nutrition. Remove any dead or withered leaves from the base, of course, and then carefully thin out, here and there, to uncover developing trusses. Keep a sharp lookout for any side shoots that you may have missed. Watch out also for blight (see June Guide) and give another spraying or dusting as a precaution.

Now is the time when the quality of plants tells. If yours are not all they should be, make a resolution to start with better stock next year. There are still too many over-forced weakly plants bought by the unwary.

3

ONIONS

A little meat goes a long way—with plenty of onions to flavour the dish. We shall need all the meat-stretching flavour we can harvest, and now is the critical time in the life of the spring-sown onion. On the care taken in lifting and ripening depends its ability to keep well in storage.

First step is to bend the tops over and then leave for about a fortnight while they shrivel. If you have some "bull-necks" which refuse to be bent, use them up in the kitchen in the next few weeks.

To lift, loosen the bulbs by pushing a fork into the soil well under them, and lever them up. Then lay the bulbs on their side with the under-surface and roots so placed as to catch the full sun. Now they must be thoroughly dried before you take them into the dry shed, spare bedroom or wherever you are going to store them.

If the month is a "baker," the process should not take long—just lay the bulbs on firm ground or on a path until the skins are really dry. If the weather alternates between dry and wet, the onions must be lifted off the soil and the most made of the sunny spells by sheltering your onions on a home-made drying frame. Prop a piece of wire netting on four corner pegs, spread the bulbs on it, then above them—about 3 in. higher—prop a sheet of corrugated iron on four more pegs. The sun, when it comes, beats on the iron and warms the onions beneath ; the air circulates freely, and the crop ripens quickly and well.

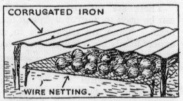

Sow Onions

See that the soil is firm, and sow fairly thickly. Use varieties of the White Spanish type or those specially recommended for autumn sowing. In the North, the first week in the month is the time : the third week is early enough down South.

Some growers divide their sowings, saving some of the seed till late December. They find that the December sowing produces fewer plants that run to seed. But whenever you sow, keep weeds firmly in check.

Hold that moisture

About 300 years ago, a scientist planted a willow shoot weighing 5 lb. in a barrel holding 200 lb. of dry soil. For five years he gave it nothing but pure water. He finished with a fine tree weighing over 169 lb. : and the soil had lost a trifling 2 oz., so he concluded that water was the "principle of vegetation."

Other scientists have since found it isn't quite as simple as that, but none of them has grown a plant without water. In fact, it takes anything up to 1,000 lb. of water to produce a single pound of plant substance.

Plants are just as thirsty in August as human beings are, though they are unable to trot into the kitchen or down the road. But they do have roots able to draw on the available moisture in the soil. It's up to us to see that the moisture gets to the roots and not into the warm air. Much can be done by timely hoeing to stop the soil cracking when it has been beaten down by heavy rains or watering. But a better way to keep the roots of peas, runner beans and tomatoes supplied with moisture is to spread a layer of half-rotted manure with plenty of straw in it, well-rotted compost material, or even decayed lawn-mowings, between the rows and around the plants. This is a mulch, but it is next to useless if you put it on already bone dry soil. Seize the moment after a fall of rain, or if the rain fails, give the ground a good soaking.

See that the mulch is open in texture : heavy impenetrable stuff keeps the air from the soil and may even tend to sour it. Watch your lawn-mowings specially. Mulching also helps to keep down the weeds.

STOP PEST NEWS

By this time in the year the patient gardener is prepared—or he should be—for anything in the nature of pests. This month's particular unpleasantness may take the form of Cabbage Aphis on the members of the cabbage family. It is easy enough to recognise. Leaves begin to curl or crinkle ; part of the leaf turns a paler green, and on the underside of the crinkled leaf is a mass of greyish-blue, powdery-looking insects busily sucking the vitality out of your plants and crippling them.

If these pests find their way into growing hearts of your young kales, sprouts or other green stuff, they may check the plants so badly that the crop will be very poor. You will probably find too that the Aphis has discovered your seedling rows of greenstuff.

The best remedy is to spray with a good nicotine insecticide, preferably one that contains soap or some other substance that acts as a "spreader" and keeps the nicotine on the leaves. Force the spray well into the hearts of the plants. Where there are large colonies, it is worth while squashing the insects with finger and thumb before spraying—if you can "take it." It is a messy business, but half measures are no good. Later sprayings at intervals of a few days will probably be necessary. The secret of control is to spray early enough and often enough.

WARNING

Nicotine and nicotine preparations are poisonous. Be sure to follow maker's directions. On Summer Cabbage almost ready for cutting, or other vegetables intended for the table within ten days, use a derris spray instead.

Help on the GREENS

Give late autumn and winter greens a light dressing of National Growmore fertiliser round each plant, raked or hoed in. Apply this now—feeding after this month will make soft growth which will not stand the severe winter weather. Keep the ground firm round winter greens or they may fail to heart-up properly.

Look after the SEEDLINGS

Give seedlings of the cabbage family and turnips a light dressing of derris dust or naphthalene dust as soon as they show through. This early treatment works better against flea beetle attack than later applications. Continue to dust with derris during growth in seed bed.

Soot for CELERY

This is a vital moment in the life of celery. Earthing-up (see June Guide) should keep up with growth. The other main needs are soot and water. Soot is the best fertiliser for the crop. The older it is, the better. It can be used on the leaves or well watered into the soil as a manure. Do not try to produce luxuriant growth—it will probably be coarse. Aim to grow short, firm, stocky plants. Never let them get dry—water must be abundant during growth.

Those POTATO HAULMS

Every year when the early potatoes have been lifted, the question is asked "What shall I do with my potato tops?" The problem is whether to put them on the compost heap or not. The answer depends on two things, namely, how good is your compost heap and how free from disease are your potato tops?

If you have had an attack of blight, or any other disease that has affected the potato tops, the answer is simple—gather them up, all of them, and burn them. If your crop has been clean and you have the sort of efficient compost heap that heats up well, there is nothing against chopping up the haulms, with a sharp spade, while they are soft and green, and treating them as any other waste. In a good compost heap they will soon rot down. The main thing about potato haulms is not to leave them lying about.

BURN ALL DISEASED HAULMS

CHOP UP AND USE SOUND HAULMS FOR COMPOST

6

Sow SPINACH . . . *the real thing*

Clever cooks, it is said, can make any vegetable into spinach. But, as with so much that cooks "make," the concoction cannot provide the health-giving benefits of the real thing. And more important, the real thing tastes better.

For winter use, sow the prickly or rough-seeded variety thinly in drills 1 in. deep and 1 ft. apart. If possible, avoid full sun. Thin to 3 in., then to 6 in. apart as plants develop. The best flavoured plants are fairly big, with broad, crisp leaves about the size of a saucer—this means proper attention to thinning.

their feet and feelers when entering or leaving the nest.

WASPS

Adjectives may relieve but they do not reduce the battalions. Traps do, especially if hung among the plum trees.

The only satisfactory way of dealing with wasps where they are causing damage to fruit is to find the nests in the neighbourhood and kill the colonies by poisoning.

There are various materials that can be used to destroy wasps in their nests. Some are dangerous in inexpert hands but ground Derris root is safe and is effective and simple to use. Put a dessert-spoonful of the powder as far into the entrance of the nest as possible, and also sprinkle a little round the entrance so that the wasps will get it on

Some people use tar, creosote or paraffin successfully. The liquid must be poured well into the nest or a soaked rag or piece of sacking pushed in by means of a stick.

The best time for dealing with wasps' nests is at dusk when most of the workers are inside. If desired, the nests may be dug out on the following day and destroyed by burning.

Trapping by means of jam-jars hung among the trees helps to reduce the population but is only a palliative. The jars should be half to three-quarters full of water into which a spoonful of jam has been stirred or a little stale beer added.

SPOONFUL OF JAM IN WATER →

FRUIT PAGE

The early varieties of dessert apples will be ready for picking this month—"Beauty of Bath," "Irish Peach" and "Gladstone." These must be picked and used as soon as they are ripe or they lose flavour. Not all the fruit ripens at the same time, so it is worth while going over the trees at intervals of a few days. There is one right way—and many wrong ways—of picking apples. The sign of ripeness is the ease with which the stalk parts company from the twig. Take the base of the apple in the palm of the hand, then raise it

until it is horizontal. If it parts easily, it is ripe. If it fails to come away easily, let it gently back to its original place and leave for a few days. The great joy about early apple varieties is that, unlike Cox's Orange Pippin and other late kinds, they do not have to mature after picking, and it is the owner's pleasure to eat them at once.

Such delights may be especially welcome if, on going over your apple trees, you find that some apples have rotted. This is probably due to Brown Rot, a disease that destroys many tons of apples every year, and also affects plums, pears, quinces and cherries. Much of this loss can be prevented. The disease starts as a mere spot, where a slight bruise, cut or insect puncture has been invaded by disease spores, carried by wind, rain or insects. The spot gradually spreads into a soft brown patch, and at the same time small swellings under the skin break through as yellowish or buff-coloured growths — or pustules — usually in concentric circles. These diseased fruits produce a crop of spores, which are carried to other fruits by flies and wasps. And so it goes on— an endless vicious cycle that can only be checked by strict hygiene on the part of growers.

Collect from apple and plum trees and under the trees, all fruit that shows the slightest sign of disease. Burn it. Go over the trees, especially the soft-wooded varieties

of apple such as "Lord Derby" and "James Grieve," and cut out all dead or dying spurs along with any cankers. Collect and burn. Keep an eye open in the winter for "mummied" fruit left on the trees— gather and burn it.

Special care is necessary when picking apples for storing. Brown Rot is liable to set in wherever there is a wound or bruise, and a favourite place of entry is the slight wound made if the stalk is torn out. So pick with the stalks on. Do not attempt to store any fruit showing signs of the disease. It will spread. And clean up under the trees. It is from mummied fruit on the trees and from rotten apples lying about that the first spore invasion usually starts.

Summer fruiting Raspberries should be pruned as soon as the last fruit has been picked. Cut out all the canes that have borne fruit. Cut them right down at ground level, leaving no snags to become resting and breeding places for pests and diseases. Burn all cut-out canes. If your canes are supported by wires, tie up the new canes, 5 or 6 in. apart, with raffia or soft string.

The same sort of treatment should be given to Blackberries and Loganberries. Cut out fruited shoots and thin out weak new growths, and any showing purplish spots (signs of the disease Cane Spot). Keep about 6 or 8 of the strongest shoots and tie them in.

CUT OUT OLD CANES

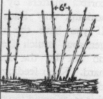

TIE UP NEW CANES

HOW TO KEEP RABBITS

THIS BOOK TELLS YOU HOW YOU CAN JOIN IN THE GOVERNMENT SCHEME TO PRODUCE MORE DOMESTIC RABBIT MEAT, FURS AND WOOL FOR YOURSELF AND FOR THE NATION

PUBLISHED BY "FUR & FEATHER, IDLE, BRADFORD, YORKS.

If you had the space, then rabbits, chickens and even pigs could be kept in the garden though many people found it hard to eat what had become a domestic pet. These hutches would not pass modern Animal Welfare regulations.

September

Apples appear again in September as an essential element of the Harvest Festival period of mists and mellow fruitfulness. 'James Grieve', 'Ellison's Orange' and 'Allington Pippin' were added to the recommended list. Cooking apples included the wonderfully named 'Crawley Beauty' and the 'Rev. W. Wilks'. Amidst the satisfying pictures of plentiful marrows and pumpkins, apples and onions came the disturbing news that a potato shortage was likely to raise its head again unless care was taken with storage. Clamps were the most common method of storage, enabling over-wintering of large quantities. This method did, however, have disadvantages with pilfering common on allotment sites, and the obvious difficulties of retrieving just a few potatoes for dinner!

Most gardeners tried to store at least some of their crop in a shed or even, in the days before central heating, a cold dark spot in the house. Dark spots in the house were in considerable demand for storing and ripening vegetables in wartime. Tomatoes which had failed to ripen on the plant needed to be brought indoors, while herbs and onions needed to be hung in a cool dry place.

As well as fitting stored produce into the house, seed for next year also had to be accommodated indoors if there was no shed on the allotment or garden. Before the development of F1 hybrids (which cannot be bred from) seed saving was common and difficulties in obtaining seed during wartime meant that most gardeners tried to save larger seeds, such as peas and beans, at the very least. Lettuce and tomato seeds were more tricky, although leek and onion seeds were easy and produced large attractive seed heads.

MINISTRY OF AGRICULTURE

ALLOTMENT &

Garden Guide

VOL. 1 No. 9   SEPTEMBER - 1945

> "O sweet September, thy first breezes bring
> The dry leaf's rustle and the squirrel's laughter
> The cool fresh air whence health and vigour spring
> And promise of exceeding joy hereafter."

LIKE the squirrel, the gardener who has done his job well can indulge in a satisfied smile in September, when he surveys the fruits of his labours and decides on those "O.S." fruits and vegetables that will represent his household at the church or chapel harvest festival, tokens of his appreciation of the world-old partnership between Providence and man. Assuming the weather has not been too unkind and the pests not too troublesome, he can smile at the abundance that will be his squirrel's store for the late autumn and winter days that lie ahead. So it is natural that this issue of the Guide should be concerned mainly with harvesting and storing.

HARVESTING & STORING

THE "INSURANCE" CROP

In view of the potato shortage this year, we should take extra care in harvesting and storing our own crops so as to avoid any risk of loss. The tops should be cut down and removed about a fortnight before lifting time—burn them if there is the slightest suspicion of blight. Choose a fine day for lifting, and leave the tubers on the ground just long enough to dry—about four or five hours.

Be careful to sort your crop, to make sure that you don't store any diseased tubers. But even with the most careful sorting, a diseased tuber or two may accidentally get mixed with sound ones. So to prevent disease spreading, sprinkle powdered lime, or a mixture of lime and flowers of sulphur, among the tubers. The sulphur also helps to keep vermin away.

Potatoes are easily damaged by even a few degrees of frost, and are then unfit for human food. If you can, stored potatoes fortnightly and remove any diseased tubers.

If you have a large crop and want to store them in a clamp or pie, this diagram may help you in building it.

Choose the driest bit of your land for your clamp and mark out a strip 3 ft. 6 in. wide and long enough to take your crop.

Don't be niggardly with the straw —provide at least a 6-in. layer. Press the lower ends of the straw close to the ground, for it is along the edge of the clamp that the frost generally creeps in. The straw layer should reach almost to the top of the

PRESS STRAW TO GROUND

6" THICK   3' 6"

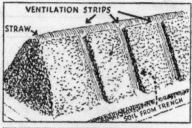

VENTILATION STRIPS

STRAW

SOIL FROM TRENCH

STRIPS FILLED IN WHEN FROST THREATENS

VENTILATION HOLES

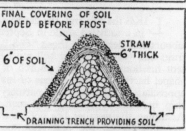

FINAL COVERING OF SOIL ADDED BEFORE FROST

STRAW 6" THICK

6" OF SOIL

DRAINING TRENCH PROVIDING SOIL

store your crops in boxes or barrels, rather than in sacks—and line the containers with old newspapers as a protection against frost. Put the boxes or barrels in a dry, frost-proof shed for the winter and cover them with old sacking, giving extra covering in severe weather.

Label your varieties and use the poorer keepers first; for instance, Arran Banner should be used before Arran Peak. Be careful about ventilation, particularly in the first months of storage; the door should be kept open, also the window when the weather permits. Look over your potatoes. You then put a covering of straw over the top of the ridge, so that its ends overlap the straw at the sides. This ensures that the rain runs down the outside and not into the clamp. To keep the straw in place, put some soil along the lower edge and a spadeful here and there over the whole of the straw covering.

Allow a few days for "perspiring," and then cover most of the straw (to within 4 in. of the top of the ridge) with 6 in. of soil, leaving 6 in. strips bare every so often. To get this soil, dig a trench 1 ft. away from the base of the clamp, about 6 in. deep. Cut an outlet in the trench to make sure that all water drains away.

When frost threatens fill in the bare strips with soil and also cover the ridge. But make ventilation holes at intervals at ground level and along the top of the ridge. Stuff these holes with straw to prevent them getting blocked with soil.

If your clamp seems to be all right, you may leave it undisturbed until February, if you like. But you should then open it when it is not freezing and inspect the contents, removing any diseased tubers and "sprouts." In remaking the clamp, take care not to bruise the potatoes, or rotting may set in.

Harvesting HARICOTS

When the pods begin to turn brown, pull up the plants, tie them in bundles by the roots and hang them in a dry, open shed to ripen thoroughly. When quite dry, shell out the seeds and store them in boxes in a cold, frost-proof shed.

Storing ONIONS

Last month's Guide dealt with ripening-off the onions. They must be thoroughly dry before storing. Onions keep best when the air can get at them freely, and the easiest way to make sure of this is to hang them up on ropes. This is a job you can do later on, when you can find the time. First remove all the roots loose skin and most of the tops. Then hang up a rope about 3 ft long, with a knot at the end, and tie a single good-sized onion to the end of it to serve as a base. For the rest of the rope, tie on four onions at a time. It is best to

the other you tie the tops to the rope by running the string round twice and finishing with a knot. Cut off the unwanted tops as you go along, but there's no need to cut the binding string. And so on up the rope, each bunch fitting snugly on top of the bunch beneath.

Some varieties of onions will not keep for long, for instance, Giant Rocca, Excelsior and Prizetaker—these should be used first. Ailsa Craig, Up-to-Date, Bedfordshire Champion and Southport Yellow Globe will last until Christmas, while

grade your onions : large onions on one rope and small onions on another. Arrange them round the rope and hold them with one hand, while with

varieties sush as James's Long Keeping, Giant Zittau, Nuneham Park and Ebenezer will last until late winter and spring.

Harvesting
MARROWS & PUMPKINS

These may be stored for winter use as vegetables and for preserving. Only fully developed and ripened fruits should be set aside for storage, and they should be handled carefully to avoid bruising the skins.

Being very susceptible to low temperatures and easily damaged by frost, these fruits need a warm, dry atmosphere, such as that of a kitchen, bedroom or attic, to ensure successful storage. Cellars and outside sheds, and other damp places where the temperature is likely to fall below 45° F., are unsuitable. From 50 to 65° F. is the most suitable tempera-ture for storage. The fruits may be placed in crates or boxes, or laid out singly on shelves, but they are best hung from the ceiling in nets.

Given this treatment, they can usually be relied upon to keep in good condition until January or February.

The harvesting of carrots, beet and certain other root crops will be dealt with in next month's Guide.

Storing TOMATOES

Mature tomatoes which are not ripened by the time the autumn frosts are coming on, may be stored separately in such receptacles as trays or box-lids, lined with a few layers of newspaper, which will help to make sure that the fruits remain where placed. Arrange the fruits in a single layer so that they do not touch one another. If there is any risk of touching, separate the rows by strips of

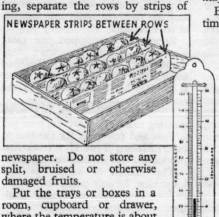

NEWSPAPER STRIPS BETWEEN ROWS

newspaper. Do not store any split, bruised or otherwise damaged fruits.

Put the trays or boxes in a room, cupboard or drawer, where the temperature is about 55° F. (not under 50° F. and preferably under 60° F.). A room where the temperature is liable to fall below 50° F. at night should, if possible, be avoided. A temperature above 60° F. may cause the tomatoes to shrivel, but is otherwise less harmful.

Store the tomatoes in the dark; but if you wish to hasten the ripening of some fruits expose them to the light at a temperature of 60-65° F. Storage in the dark tends to prolong the period of storing, and so the period during which tomatoes are available may be appreciably extended.

Examine the fruits from time to time, and remove any that have ripened or any that begin to show signs of decay.

Storing tomatoes in peat or sawdust is not recommended. Sawdust sometimes imparts an unpleasant flavour, and both peat and sawdust are difficult to maintain at the right degree of dryness. It should be remembered that though very dry conditions may cause shrivelling, appreciable moisture favours the growth of moulds, which will develop quickly under the slight warmth that is otherwise conducive to the keeping of tomatoes. For this reason, storing in the moist warmth of the kitchen is inadvisable.

Green, immature fruits may be used for chutney and pickles.

Harvesting your own saved SEED

In the July Guide there was a section devoted to saving your own seed, and we promised that in a later issue we would tell you how to harvest it. The only "safe" vegetables for seed saving by the amateur are peas, beans, onions, leeks, tomatoes, lettuce, ridge cucumbers and marrows, so this note will be restricted to them.

PEAS AND BEANS

If only a pound or two of seed is being saved, leave the pods until nearly dry. The seed at this stage should be firm and tough ; pressure with the finger nail should not easily cut the skin but only dent it.

TESTING SKIN OF BEAN FOR RIPENESS

To finish the drying, pick off the pods and spread them in a thin layer in a dry, airy place. When the seeds are quite hard, shell them from the pods and store in cotton or paper bags.

If your space is limited, the seeds may be shelled from the pods as soon as they are taken from the plant, and dried by spreading them in a thin layer on a tray. Move them each day so that they are all exposed to the air in turn.

ONIONS & LEEKS

Onion seed is usually fit to harvest by September, leeks in October. The seed should be black and doughy, not watery, before harvesting. If the stem below the head turns yellow, or some of the capsules burst open, the head is then certainly safe to cut. Cut off the heads with 12 in. or more of stem attached, and lay them in a sunny, airy place to dry. Place the onion heads in a bag since the dry seeds easily fall out.

Leeks take a long time to dry and the capsules remain tough. The easiest way to deal with very small quantities of leeks is to rub the heads on a fine sieve. If the threshed seeds and chaff are placed in water, the

good seeds will sink and the chaff and poor seeds will float. Do not let the seeds remain more than a few minutes in water ; dry them immediately by spreading in a thin layer on a dish in an airy place.

POOR SEED & CHAFF

WATER

GOOD SEED

TOMATOES

At least 10 lb. of tomatoes are required to produce 1 oz. of seed. Remove from the fruit the pulp containing the seeds and put it in a jar to ferment. After two or three days, tip it into a fine sieve and wash it vigorously under the tap ; the pulp will wash away from the seeds, which may then be spread on muslin to dry.

LETTUCE

Keep close watch for the moment when the seed heads are ripe, since loss of seed results from shattering and from the ravages of birds. Inspect the plants at frequent intervals and pluck off any heads that show a "downy" formation. This usually appears within about a fortnight of flowering. Finish drying the heads on a tray under cover.

MARROWS AND RIDGE CUCUMBERS

Leave the fruit intended for seed on the plant until it is fully ripe. The seed should be removed by hand, washed to remove the surrounding pulp and dried in the sun.

PARSLEY "TIP"

You may now find your spring-sown parsley running to seed, some of it in full flower. These flower stems will exhaust the plant. So your best plan is to cut down the plants almost to ground level and give them a little fertiliser and some water. By this means you can have fine parsley all through the winter.

Those SPRING CABBAGES

Thinking about next year brings us to the need for adequate supplies of winter greens. September is the month for planting out spring cabbages, and every available piece of ground should be devoted to this valuable vitamin-giving vegetable. When the onions have been removed and the ground has been lightly hoed, dusted with lime and well raked, spring cabbages may be planted in rows 1 ft. 6 in. to 2 ft apart, allowing 1 ft. between each plant. This is somewhat closer than is usually recommended for spring cabbages; but as the cabbages grow in the spring each alternate plant may be cut and used as spring greens, leaving the remaining plants ample room to develop into fine-hearting specimens for cutting in May and early June. Any surplus seedlings remaining in the seed beds should be thinned out to 2 or 3 in. apart, to form a reserve store that may be planted out on vacant ground next March or April, so providing a succession to those planted out this autumn. These later plants come into bearing when the main crop is finished and provide useful cabbages in early summer.

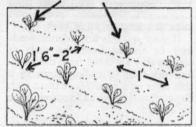

ALTERNATIVE PLANTS FOR CUTTING AS SPRING GREENS

What about TURNIP TOPS?

At this time of the year, it is well worth while to sow a row or two of turnips, not with the idea of producing roots, but to get a supply of green tops for use next spring. The seeds should be sown very thinly in rows 1 ft. apart. When the seedlings appear, thin fairly lightly in the early stages, as the plants have to undergo the winter and bad weather and pests may make inroads on them. Later on they may be thinned again, as the plants require more room to develop. The variety Green Top Stone is very suitable for sowing to produce a supply of tasty, green leaves that will be valuable as an extra green crop in the difficult month of April.

BEET "tip"

Look at a sample root or two in your beet rows. You may find that some are getting old and "ringy." If you sowed the seeds early in the year, it is quite possible that the beet are ready for lifting and would be much better lifted now and stored in damp sand or soil in an odd corner outdoors. The main crop should still be growing well at the moment, but some earlier roots may go past their best if left in the ground any longer.

FRUIT from the GARDEN

The shortage of fruit during the war has led many people to turn their minds in the direction of growing their own, especially apples. They have grown vegetables successfully, and feel they can grow fruit, too. Why not, if they have got the necessary space for a tree or two and perhaps some bush fruit ? So here are a few notes about apple growing.

should know this, for the root-stock has a marked influence on the growth of the tree, and so on the age at which it will start to bear. If the root-stock is vigorous, growth will also be vigorous, you will have to do much pruning and fruit-bearing will be delayed ; if, on the other hand, the tree has been propagated on a weaker growing root-stock, such as

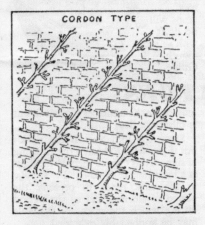

CORDON TYPE

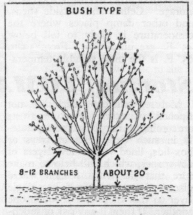

BUSH TYPE

8-12 BRANCHES   ABOUT 20"

The aim should be to plant the compact, restricted type of tree that is easy to handle, gives a quick return and takes up very little space. So keep to the cordon type or the bush tree. The cordon has a single straight stem, furnished with fruiting spurs along its entire length. It is the type for planting against a wall or a fence. The bush tree has a stem of about 20 in. before branching takes place, and eight to twelve branches grow in the form of a cup, leaving an open centre. This form should be chosen when planting in the open garden.

A cordon tree should be at least two or three years old when you buy it, since a tree of this age will already be furnished with fruit buds. A bush tree should be about four years.

Be careful when you buy fruit trees. Apples are propagated by budding or grafting scions of the selected variety on special root-stocks. It is important that you

Type IX, growth will be less strong and the tree will come into bearing at an early age.

Reputable nurserymen use root-stocks whose habit is known ; such root-stocks have been classified accordingly. So if your garden soil is in good heart and fertile, ask the nurseryman to supply apples on Malling Type IX, which is a weak growing stock. If, however, your soil is light and poor, ask for the tree to be on Malling Type II, a stock that produces a tree of medium vigour.

The choice of variety is also important, for any particular variety behaves differently in different localities. For instance, Cox's Orange—possibly the most famous English dessert apple—does best in the south and in areas of low rainfall. It is not a good variety for planting in cold or wet districts. People's tastes differ, too. The small gardener would do well to take the advice of his County

Horticultural Superintendent or his local horticultural society about suitable varieties for local conditions. Here is a list of a few well-known varieties that can generally be relied on to do well in most districts, though some may not suit every condition throughout the country.

Dessert apples	Cooking apples
James Grieve	*Rev. W. Wilks
*Ellison's Orange	Lord Derby
Allington Pippin	Lane's Prince Albert
Laxton's Superb	*Crawley Beauty

The varieties marked with a * are self-fertile, and Crawley Beauty flowers very late, so being specially suited to districts subject to late frosts. If there is room for only one apple tree choose a self-fertile variety. Where two or more varieties are to be grown, select those that flower about the same time.

Planting operations will be dealt with in a later Guide.

If you would like more information than can be supplied in this Guide about how to increase fruit production in the garden, you would find the Ministry's bulletin "Fruit from the Garden" very helpful. You can get it for 3d. (4d. post free), either through any bookseller, or direct from H.M. Stationery Office, York House, Kingsway, London, W.C.2.

Plant Certified Stocks

Good planting stock costs very little more than rubbish and in the long run it will prove *less* costly. Many of you will have been disappointed with the crops produced by those fruit bushes and plants that you have picked up cheap. You may be lucky now and again, but cheap stocks rarely give satisfaction. They will possibly introduce diseases and pests into your garden, and often they do not prove true to type. The best plan is to plant stocks that are certified true to variety and substantially free from pests and diseases.

Every season the Ministry of Agriculture examines stocks of strawberry plants and blackcurrant bushes, and issues certificates for those stocks that attain the standards laid down. The supply of certified stocks is limited, but it is worth while saying to your nurseryman, when you order, "Certified Stocks, please!" And you will find' that certified stocks please.

Issued by the Ministry of Agriculture and Fisheries, Berri Court Hotel, St. Annes, Lytham St. Annes Lancs.

Wt. T8866/8677 125M 7/4 CN&CoLtd

*Potatoes were easy and popular to grow and Potato Pete
had his own cookbook and advertising campaign.*

October

Although a few people still clamp potatoes now, it would be rare indeed to see a clamp of carrots! And yet the wonderful igloo shape shown in the October Guide would complement any vegetable patch. Buried under sand, 6 inches of straw and 6-8 inches of soil, the carrots should survive even the hardest frost, although (as with potatoes) once the clamp was broken for spring use, then it was difficult to re-form. It was recommended that beetroot should be sealed in boxes or barrels of sand in a shed, making them slightly easier to access but raising serious questions about the sheer quantities of sand gardeners were expected to get hold of, and the strength of shed floors!

Lime was second only to sand in the quantities used. An essential chemical in the liberation of other important soil nutrients, lime was imputed with almost mystical powers and added in liberal quantities to any vegetable plot. There was even a specific government department set up to monitor supplies and pricing. Despite this, lime, and in particular the favoured hydrated lime, soon ran short during wartime and gardeners were urged to use ground limestone or chalk instead.

Liming is still carried out by any serious gardener who wants to grow brassicas and root vegetables on tired or sandy soils, but it is rare now to see novice gardeners anxiously turning their plots white at every opportunity. Modern gardeners anxious as to whether their plots need lime might buy a cheap and easy home-testing kit but readers of the Guides were reduced to asking the local Parks Superintendent or Horticultural Secretary for advice. Most of them probably went ahead and added some lime anyway 'just in case'.

MINISTRY OF AGRICULTURE

ALLOTMENT &

Garden Guide

VOL. 1 No. 10   OCTOBER - 1945

> "Hail, old October, bright and chill,
> First freedman from the summer sun !
> Spice high the bowl and drink your fill !
> Thank Heaven, at last the summer's done ! "

An American divine wrote that October is nature's funeral month and that the month of departure is more beautiful than the month of coming : that October is more beautiful than May. Gardeners may well argue about that, but they will agree that the sun of their gardening year is setting in October. It is a time for reflection, for a judicial summing up of our successes and failures.

Are our failures due to any lack in ourselves ? Did we fail to tackle those pests in good time or did those poor, worthless crops result from a lack of fertility in our soil ? The farmer, we are told, looks at winter with spring in his eyes. So does the good gardener. For both the practical couplet is this : "In October dung your field,
And your land its wealth shall yield."
But the reader may say, "It's all very well for the farmer, but where can I get dung ? " Well, the answer to that has been given many many times : it is simply this—if you can't get dung, make compost. And how few gardeners do, yet compost will help them to keep their land fertile.

THAT COMPOST

October is the picture month— the month for painted leaves, as Thoreau, the American nature writer called it. That's a nice poetic thought, but to the sensible gardener those painted leaves, when they drop, become compost. Leaves of oak, beech and birch are very valuable for the compost heap, but pine and spruce needles, together with lime and plane tree leaves, are best burnt and the ashes used instead as a fertiliser.

Don't make the mistake of piling masses of fallen leaves and autumnal garden waste on the heap that you may have started several months ago. Start a fresh heap, turning back to the March Guide for advice. Turn over the old heap now, and any material that has not rotted completely should be placed on the inside of the new heap, the properly decomposed stuff going to the outside.

CLEAR THAT RUBBISH

Clearing up the garden or allotment is a job that should not be put off. If decaying vegetable material, old sticks, cabbage stumps and other rubbish is left to rot in the garden, all kinds of pests and vermin will be encouraged. Keep up with the work of clearing the ground as soon as the crops are finished. Put all suitable material on the compost heap, while not forgetting the needs of any domestic livestock.

Bean sticks can often be made to serve two seasons, if they are care-fully stored and kept dry during the winter. Pea sticks of the brushwood type are seldom much use after one season and should be burned.

RUBBISH HARBOURS PESTS

THOSE BONFIRES

Keep them to the smallest limits and burn only woody or diseased material, the underground parts of thistles, docks, couch grass and the like.

Bonfire ash should not be left out for the rain and dew to dissolve and wash away the very soluble form of potash it contains. It can be incorporated in the garden soil immediately it is cold, or it may be bagged, stored in a dry place and used as a fertilizer when needed.

More about STORING

CARROTS

The main carrot crop should now be ready for lifting. Treat the roots carefully, lifting with a fork and taking care not to damage roots or crown. Trim off the leaves near the crown, but do not cut the top part of the carrot, even if it is green. Some gardeners slash off the top half-inch, but that leads to trouble later on when the carrots are stored. Any split, misshapen, forked roots, or those that show signs of damage by carrot fly or other pests, should be kept out for use in the next few weeks. The rest can be stored, either indoors, or, if you have more than you can conveniently store under cover, you could clamp them as you would potatoes — (see September Guide).

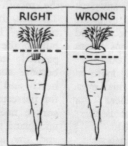

2

Carrots stored indoors can best be kept in boxes. A layer of dry sand, soil or ashes should be placed over the bottom of the box or other container, then a layer of carrots completely covered with sand, and so on until the box is full.

Clamping outside is very simple. Make a level site, preferably in the shade, and place the carrots, thick end to the outside, in the form of a circle. Lay a few carrots in the middle and sprinkle a little sand over them to level up ; then put a second layer of carrots on the top of the first, and so on. The circular layers get a little narrower each time until the whole heap builds up into a shapely cone. Cover the cone with a layer of 4 to 6 in. of straw. Then dig out about a foot of soil around the heap, to get sufficient to cover the clamp to a depth of 6 to 8 in. Leave ventilation holes at the top, filling them with twists of straw that show through the soil. Otherwise cover the whole clamp with soil before severe weather sets in. It may be necessary later on to add a little more soil to the outer covering, but 8 in. should provide enough protection in a reasonably mild winter.

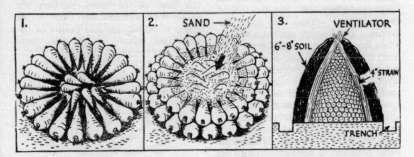

BEETS

Beetroots, too, must be lifted before frost seriously threatens. The leaves are twisted off—not cut—and the roots taken inside to store. This is better than trying to store them in clamps in the open. They should be buried in boxes or barrels of sand, ashes or finely-sifted soil. Whatever material you use should not be bone dry ; while it should be moderately dry, the roots may shrivel if it is quite dry. The boxes of roots should be stood in a shed, cellar or store of some kind that is frostproof. A storage temperature of between 30° and 35°F. is most suitable. The important point to remember is that the beet must be kept free from frost. During hard frosts, if the store is not frostproof, an additional covering of old sacks, bracken, straw or something of a similar nature, should be heaped over and around the boxes. Stored in this way the roots will keep for many months.

About those ARTICHOKES

Some readers may be wondering if Jerusalem artichokes should be lifted like potatoes. That is not necessary; indeed, they keep better in the ground if, in very severe weather, a covering of leaves or bracken is heaped over the roots. The stems should be cut down now and bruised and put on the compost heap, but the roots may stop in the ground until after Christmas. Most gardeners lift the tubers in February and replant some for next year. Those intended for the kitchen are then stored in damp sand and can be kept fresh for several months.

Picking BRUSSELS ... a tip

Early-planted Brussels sprouts should now be ready for picking. There is a right way and a wrong way of gathering them. Start at the bottom and clear the stem of sprouts as they become large enough; don't pick a sprout here and there, but do it systematically from the bottom of the

stem. Some gardeners are doubtful whether they should remove the growing tuft of leaves at the top of the plant. That should be left until next spring, for the leaves are necessary to the health of the plant and also afford protection from the weather.

A LEEK tip

A little soil should be drawn up to leek plants now to encourage them to produce sizeable, well-blanched stems.

Getting early RHUBARB

Forced or early rhubarb is one of the things we can enjoy in these difficult days when delicacies are none too plentiful. If you have some good crowns or clumps of rhubarb, you can, without much trouble, provide the table with early stalks. When the plants have shed their summer leaves, place some dry leaves or bracken loosely over the crowns. A box or big pot should be placed over this material, to keep it dry and stop it blowing about. This encourages the rhubarb to make early growth. If you have a dark shed or a greenhouse, you can lift a few crowns and place them on the shed floor or under the greenhouse staging. Hang sacking in front of the staging to make it dark. Crowns intended for such treatment can be lifted a week or so before they are taken inside. They should be stood on the surface of the soil and if a slight frost occurs, so much the better, it will make them break into growth earlier.

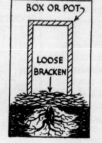

BOX OR POT

LOOSE BRACKEN

This LIMING business

Much of our land is in need of lime. Every year the soil loses lime steadily and continuously. The rate of loss varies with the circumstances, but in industrial areas there is a special need for lime because of the acid ingredients in smoke and fumes from factories and business plants.

Gradual loss of lime makes the soil become acid and sour—and more so as time goes on. Now lime is an essential plant food; unless the soil contains it in suitable quantity, it is not possible to grow good crops.

SHEEPS SORREL

Most cultivated crops dislike sour soil, except potatoes, which can stand it unless it is very acid. Turnips and swedes, for instance, are both unreliable on such soils and are less capable of withstanding drought and pest attacks. "Finger-and-Toe" or "Club-Root" also indicates the need for lime, as does a heavy soil that shows an excessive stickiness, a tendency to set hard and a difficulty in getting a good tilth. But light, sandy soils lose their lime very quickly, and it is on such soils that troubles from sourness are most common and acute. The presence of certain weeds, such as spurrey, sheep's sorrel and corn marigold, is one of the

CLUBROOT

best indications of a lack of lime.

Some allotment holders and gardeners have perhaps found it difficult to get the kind of lime they need for their land. Perhaps they put in an order months in advance of liming time and still found they could not get delivery in time. Probably they ordered hydrated lime and would not be satisfied with anything else. So they went without—and their crops suffered. That was a mistake, for other kinds of lime are just as beneficial as hydrated lime, if applied at the proper rate.

CORN MARIGOLD

Some readers, remembering the science of their schooldays, may like to know a bit more about "lime." The word is commonly used to mean not only calcium oxide (quicklime), but also calcium hydroxide (slaked or hydrated lime) and calcium carbonate (limestone and chalk). Though quicklime used to be by far the most common form of lime bought by farmers, carbonate of lime is gaining considerable popularity and is now as much sought after as quicklime and its derivatives —ground and hydrated lime. Quicklime is obtained from either chalk or limestone burnt in a lime kiln. This is generally in lumps or it may be further processed by crushing to form ground burnt lime, or still further by the addition of a controlled amount of water to form calcium hydroxide (slaked or hydrated lime). The last is always in a fine state of division, easily stored, and probably for that reason has been much in demand by gardeners. The other form of lime that is more suitable for storage is carbonate of lime, which may be limestone or chalk (really a soft limestone) both ground to a fine powder. Quality depends to a great extent on the pureness of the rock from which lime is derived.

The demands for hydrated lime are much greater than the supply. This shortage affects farmers as well as allotment holders and gardeners, and is due to the fact that other vital industries—especially the building trade—need most of the hydrated lime produced to-day. What can the gardener or allotment holder do if he cannot get his little bit of "hydrated"? The answer to that is try finely ground limestone or chalk. Both are equally effective as hydrated when applied in the appropriate quantities necessary to correct the sourness of the soil. Hydrated costs nearly twice as much as ground limestone ; on the other hand it is necessary to put on one and a half times as much ground limestone as hydrated. Both ground limestone and chalk are fairly readily obtainable compared with hydrated lime.

It does not follow from what has already been said that all gardens and allotments need lime. The only sure way of finding out what is lacking in the soil is to have it tested. The local Parks Superintendent, the secretary of the district allotments or horticultural society or some knowledgeable neighbour would advise how this can be done.

On planting FRUIT TREES

In the September Guide we dealt with the sort of fruit to grow in the small garden and promised later on to supply information about planting. Here it is.

First of all, the site. Peaches and pears need abundant sunshine. Most other fruits do best in a sunny position, but are not so particular and often succeed in partial shade.

Peaches or pears should go on the south wall or fence, apples and plums on the west or east, and morello cherries on the north. Black currants, gooseberries and raspberries should be in a bed where they can be netted against bird attack. Loganberries or blackberries should be trained on a boundary fence.

In the open garden you could plant one or more dwarf bush apples or gooseberry, red or black currant bushes. Apples planted about 10 to 15 ft. apart in a square could have a gooseberry or currant bush placed in the centre.

As fruit trees and bushes have to

BASTARD TRENCHING

Break up and turn over subsoil, add manure, and then move topsoil A to B

grow on the same piece of ground for several years, you must cultivate the plot thoroughly and deeply. The best method is bastard trenching, breaking up the sub-soil as far as possible. Do this over the whole fruit plot—especially on heavy soils— not just where the tree or bush is to stand.

As to manure, the general rule is that bush fruits need much bulky organic stuff, which provides the soil with plenty of humus (see January Guide). Through generous manuring the moisture is retained near the surface and close to the shallow roots of bush fruits. Use farmyard manure, if you can get it; if not, you could use good stuff from the compost heap, decayed lawn clippings or similar material. Apply between the first and second spits when bastard trenching. When planting cordon apples give similar treatment, making the border so treated 3 ft. wide. In the open garden, if the soil is in an average state of fertility, no special treatment is needed and no bulky manure should be applied, since this would hasten growth and delay fruiting.

When you come to planting, use a line to keep the rows straight and put in sticks to show the position of each tree or bush. Provided the weather is not frosty, you can plant at any time between late autumn and the end of March, but, if possible, plant in late autumn. Don't plant when the ground is too wet or too sticky; wait until it is reasonably dry and workable. If the weather is frosty when you get your trees or bushes, cover the roots with soil and wait until you can plant out.

Cordon apples are usually planted 2 ft. to 3 ft. apart in the row, while bush apples on dwarf stocks are given

10 ft. 5 ft. apart each way is the distance for gooseberry and currant bushes, while raspberry canes should be placed 18 in. apart with 6 ft. between the rows. If you are planting cordon gooseberries or red currants, allow 1 ft. apart.

For the rest of this note it is proposed to deal with the planting of cordon and bush apples. When the time is right, take out enough soil to make a hole wide and deep enough to allow the roots to be evenly spread out. In planting cordon apples it is generally better to take out a fairly wide shallow trench along the entire row. Cut back any coarse or injured roots on tree or bush, using an upward sloping cut. Set the tree in the hole and spread the roots out evenly. In planting against a wall or fence keep the stem about 6 in. away from it. Sprinkle some fine soil over the roots. If there is more than one layer of roots, hold up the upper roots. Work the soil well into the spaces between the lower roots, and when they are covered, tread the soil firmly. Keep on filling and treading until the hole is completely filled in. Firm planting is very important, but

do not plant any deeper than the tree or bush was planted in the nursery : you can usually judge this by the ring of soil adhering to the stem. Complete your planting by giving a mulch of farmyard manure or compost.

Cordon apples are not set upright, but sloping at an angle of about 45°. If your rows run north to south, keep the roots to the south, with the top of the tree sloping north. When the rows run east to west, the slope of the trees is not so important.

Bush apples on Malling IX root stock (see September Guide) need staking with a stout stake, which should be driven in about 2 ft. from the base of the stem, so that the stake rests against the stem at an angle of about 45° and points in the direction from which the wind generally comes. The stake should

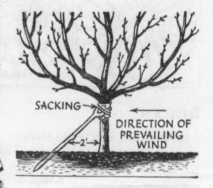

be driven in securely until the top just comes to rest against the stem below the lowest branch. Wrap a bit of sacking round the stem at the top, so as to prevent the tree being chafed, and then tie stem and stake together with a strong cord.

The pruning of newly-planted fruit trees and bushes will be touched on in a later Guide.

Issued by the
MINISTRY OF
AGRICULTURE AND
FISHERIES

Wt. T11113/8691 125M 7/4 CN&CoLtd.

*Virtually whatever their age, children were encouraged
to help out with tasks in the garden.*

November

November is a difficult month for the gardener, and for the garden writer! Crops are safely harvested, apart from those few that will over-winter, sowing is finished for the year, and it is still too early to be excited about the spring push. The *Allotment & Garden Guide* fell back on the time-honoured tasks of 'getting on with the digging', cleaning up the plot, winter pruning and the inevitable spraying of chemicals. Clearing up weeds led to discussion of the compost heap, and it is surprising that many readers still needed encouragement and instruction on making what is now a commonplace component of any garden.

Shortage of manure and fertilisers after the outbreak of war had meant that gardeners were encouraged to try making their own compost from what little waste was left after the pigs, hens and rabbits had had their bit. Compost heaps were first reported on in *The Times* in the late autumn of 1939, when a Mr Howard described their use in India. Since then they had been the subject of much discussion in the gardening press and a special Dig for Victory Leaflet (No. 7) had been distributed to help newcomers to understand the concept. This leaflet was still available in 1945 and had been recommended in the March *Allotment & Garden Guide*, alongside another article on compost making.

MINISTRY OF ··· AGRICULTURE

ALLOTMENT &

Garden Guide

VOL. 1 No. 11   **NOVEMBER · 1945**

"No warmth, no cheerfulness, no
    healthful ease,
No comfortable feel in any member,—
No shade, no shine, no butterflies,
    no bees,
No fruits, no flowers, no leaves, no
    birds—November ! "

NOVEMBER may not be as
gloomy as Tom Hood—who
sang the Song of the Shirt—has
painted it ; but it has never been
a popular month, least of all to
gardeners. For the perennial border
may look bedraggled and the vegetable plot untidy and a bit sombre.
We may have some promising looking
beds of winter greens to reassure us
that there will be no hungry gap in
the early part of next year. But
we shall miss the colour and interest
associated with our runner beans
and peas, our beet and carrots ;
while our fruit trees will be "bare
ruin'd choirs where late the sweet
birds sang."

We shall miss the bees—our
pollinating allies. We shall miss the
butterflies—at least the beautifully
coloured sorts. There is nothing
to fear from them : in fact, some
of them are beneficial : for instance,
the Small Tortoiseshell, Red Admiral
and Peacock thrive on stinging
nettles. But we shall be glad to
see the back of that beastly pest
the "Cabbage White" butterfly, for
this year saw the biggest invasion
from the Continent since 1940, and
one Lincolnshire schoolboy of eleven
alone killed about 3,700 with a
branch of a bush.

Well, there's very little we can
do this month about the vegetable

plot, except to do a spot of tidying up; ordering our farmyard manure— if we are lucky enough to have a source of supply—and getting on with digging such bare land as there may be; and checking up on our stored crops to make sure they are keeping well. But given the right sort of weather we can do some useful work on the fruit plot.

Cleaning up

Now is the time of the year for a little bit of "garden hygiene." A bit high falutin' that term? Well, it simply means keeping the garden clean. Cleanliness, we are told, is next to godliness, and that applies to gardens and allotments as well as to persons. An unclean body—inside or outside—is asking for trouble of some sort, and an unclean vegetable plot means harbouring pests and encouraging disease. Pests and diseases have to winter somewhere, and if they don't find their quarters in cracks in the wall or the fence or on trees or shrubs, they may take them up on those beansticks that ought to have

been put away for another season, or in the rubbish pile, or among those decaying brassica leaves. So let's have a good clean up and make things tidy, putting all suitable waste on the compost heap and burning all the rest. Don't forget that the ash contains potash and should be stored away in some dry place for future use.

And when you can, stir up the soil by hoeing between the plants still on the plot, for later on this will not be feasible and it is important that you should let the air and what sun there is get into the soil to make it warm and in better condition for the roots. Weeds may have to be kept down by hand weeding; they must not be allowed to compete with your food plants.

USE SUITABLE
WASTE FOR
COMPOST

BURN OTHER REFUSE OVER TRENCH
- COLLECT ASH & STORE IN DRY PLACE

That early DIGGING

Does early digging pay? Well, many of us allotment holders and gardeners were pretty late in starting our gardening offensive this year and have been trying to catch up ever since. Perhaps because of a late start we sowed our onions too late and have regretted it. If we get a wet sticky winter—or our land is frost or snow-bound for many weeks, we may well regret later on that we didn't make a start with our digging in the late autumn when we had a chance to

get out on the plot. Of course, on really well-cropped gardens and allotments there won't be much bare ground we can dig at this time of year. But we can tackle the bare spaces from which we have taken our potatoes, runner beans, carrots and turnips.

To the "digger" with a clay or very heavy soil, early digging is a necessity. On sandy or very light soil it is less important. Turning up the heavy stuff and leaving it rough gives Nature the chance to do her work; frost, wind and rain work on the heavy lumps, making them loose and friable —easily crumbled—and so much easier to work when sowing and planting time comes along.

When digging the heavy land, work in plenty of humus—making material such as strawy manure—if you are lucky enough to have it—or compost, that will help to make the soil lighter, warmer and better aerated. On the light soils it is not usually wise to dig in manure at this time of year, since there is a danger that much of the plant food it contains will be washed to lower levels by the winter rains and so be lost to the plant.

Many of us are now worried about the problem of keeping our land fertile and in good heart, after flogging it for years during the war. We can't expect to get much manure, if any, from farmers, who likewise have their fertility problems. Our only solution is compost. If we have not already realised this, we can now start a compost heap, for there should be plenty of material available, especially fallen leaves. The way to make compost was described in an earlier guide (March), so it will not be repeated here. If you need further information, you can still get a free Dig for Victory Leaflet No. 7—"How to make a Compost Heap" from the Ministry at Berri Court Hotel, St. Annes, Lytham St. Annes, Lancs.

Facts about WEEDS

Gardeners may argue about whether weeds or pests are their chief headache. Pests we have dealt with pretty fully in earlier Guides and it may not be out of place here to say a few words about weeds, for a wet autumn may have brought us another crop, though we kept our plots fairly clean all summer. Now we may be doing a bit of digging we can dig in the annual weeds, but we must be careful to dig up and burn such perennials as dandelions, bindweed, thistles, docks and couch. Most gardeners know the serious objections to weeds, but for those who don't, here they are. Weeds absorb from the soil moisture and plant food that would otherwise nourish and increase the vegetable or fruit crop. They crowd the crop and keep from it the sunlight so essential for healthy growth; they prevent the air circu-

lating freely among the plants, and they harbour and favour insect pests and fungus diseases.

But as a writer in *The Times* said nearly forty years ago, "Many a casual gardener owes what success he has largely to the accident of weeds. They demand the use of the hoe; and the more soils and plants are studied, the more manifest does it become that a friable, well-worked surface is the prime secret of cultivation, even in the case of things that grow deep."

The most obvious way to suppress weeds is to stop them seeding. And what trouble we should save ourselves if we did—and if all our neighbours did likewise! For many weed plants produce several thousand seeds. And the seeds of many weeds do not all germinate at the same time and may

3

lie dormant in the soil and come up after many years. A single dandelion flower turns to about 170 seeds, but an established three-year-old plant produces nearly 5,000 seeds. But the groundsel beats that figure by 1,000. The pretty little blue-flowered Eyebright can score 5,000, though the common dock easily beats that, for a fair specimen can easily carry 13,000 seeds. Hence the everlasting fight against weeds with hand and hoe and weed-killer.

On the other hand, on light soils, from which plant food is washed away by autumn and winter rains, it is a good plan to let *annual* weeds grow on patches from which crops have been lifted and are remaining bare for some time. The weeds take up the plant food and store it; and when they are dug in in the spring, they give it up again by rotting away.

ONE DOCK WEED CAN PRODUCE 13,000 SEEDS

Checking up on STORED CROPS

In November, and right throughout the winter for as long as they last, look, from time to time, at your crops in store to make sure they are keeping in good condition. First, the things you can easily get at—the shallots and onions. You may find that some of your shallots have gone soft or have started growing again. This may be due either to faulty drying or to bad storage conditions: the atmosphere may be too moist or hot. Look at every bulb, removing any that have gone bad. Use first those that have begun to grow. Put the rest away in a cool, dry place protected from the frost.

If for similar reasons some of your onions are starting to sprout, they need not be considered a total loss, for they will at least provide a useful supply of fresh green tops, if handled in the right way. If you've got a greenhouse or frame, you could set the "sprouters" in a box of dry sand or ashes and encourage them to grow

on. Or they will grow on the window sill indoors. And don't forget to use first your bull-necked onions or those that weren't properly ripened.

Your tomatoes in store may also be a bit of trouble. They may be ripening too fast or not ripening at all. Or some may have gone rotten through being stored with split skins. Those that are ripening too quickly can be held back a bit by putting them in a cooler place (but not below 50°F). The backward fruits could be put for a time on the window-sill or into a warm, airy cupboard.

Your parsnips will be all right left in the ground until early March, when you can lift those that remain and store them by burying in soil or sand in a shed or outhouse, to check them from starting into growth again. But have a look at your beet, carrots and turnips in store and take out any showing signs of rot. Small lots of potatoes in sacks or boxes should also be "vetted"; those in clamp or pie are more difficult to inspect and must run some risk, though if you examine them well before clamping—and built the clamp properly—you can afford to rest content. Never open up a clamp in frosty weather.

USE SPROUTING & BULL-NECKED ONIONS FIRST

EXAMINE TOMATOES

LOOK FOR ROT IN BEET CARROTS & TURNIPS

'VET' POTATOES IN SACKS & BOXES

Eking out those WINTER GREENS

Here are a few hints that may help to eke out your supplies of winter greens on the plot. While you still have late cabbages of your own growing, or you can still buy a fairly good selection of vegetables, leave your own kales, sprouting broccoli and savoys for as long as you can, so narrowing the gap until next season's crops begin to come in. With kale, cut the top of the plant first for consumption. The stem pushes out short shoots that should be picked off for use, and this encourages other shoots to grow and provide supplies until quite late April or even into May. The sprouting broccoli shoots are made at the point where the leaves join the stem, and as these are picked further shoots are made that keep things going for quite a long time.

Don't be tempted to lift your leeks too soon just to make variety in your diet ; leave them to grow, for they will keep quite well where they are until March or April, when you may be glad of them.

Some war-time gardeners seem to be doubtful whether the tops of Brussels sprout plants make good eating. They do—at the right time. But it's not wise to cut them at this time of the season because they are necessary to the plant's growth and

in severe weather will protect the sprouts below. March is quite early enough for Brussels tops.

Spinach beet should be allowed to rest now so that it can gather strength for next spring's push. Clear the plants of leaves at the last picking, and "pick" the stems rather than cut them, since a broken end seems better able to resist the downward spread of rot than if you cut it.

PICK SPINACH BEET—<u>DON'T CUT IT</u>

Spinach beet is pretty hardy, but a severe winter can put paid to it. So if the weather looks like being hard, give the stripped plants some protection, such as straw or bracken.

USE STRAW OR BRACKEN

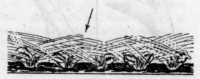

Work on the FRUIT PLOT

The value of the fruit we can grow in our own gardens needs no emphasis at this critical time. And we can grow more and better fruit if we give more attention to pruning and spraying at the right times. With much less to do on the vegetable plot, we can turn our hands to the fruit plot and get going. In so many private gardens pests and diseases play havoc with the fruit and we can do much to control them by spraying. But first, here are a few hints about winter pruning, though you would get a better idea of the art by watching some knowledgeable person do the job a time or two.

WINTER PRUNING

Before beginning to prune apples and pears, look for two kinds of shoots —"leaders" and "laterals," and two kinds of buds—"fruit buds" and "wood buds."

"Leader" shoots are the main shoot growths that extend at the ends of the branches; "laterals" are the side shoots that grow out from the "leaders." The "wood buds" that form leafy shoots are thin and pointed, while the "fruit buds" that form blossom are plump and round (see illustrations).

Cordon and dwarf bush trees are pruned by cutting back all laterals to three of four buds (see illustrations) and cutting the leaders so as to leave two-thirds of the current season's growth. Make the cut just above an outside bud. The right and wrong ways of making these cuts are shown in the pictures. If you are planting new trees this winter, pruning is best left until the buds begin to swell. Then cut all laterals back to four or five buds and reduce leaders by half.

Don't prune stone fruits unless absolutely necessary, owing to the risk of disease. In fact, plums and damsons need very little winter pruning. Dead wood should be removed, and any branches or shoots that cross or crowd should be thinned out.

Gooseberries and redcurrants can be pruned now. Winter pruning of gooseberry bushes consists of thinning

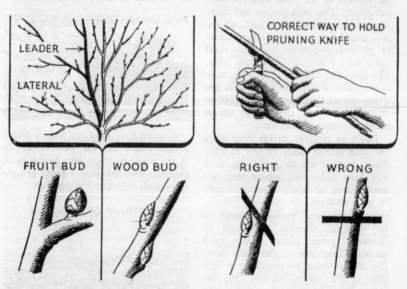

LEADER

LATERAL

FRUIT BUD   WOOD BUD

CORRECT WAY TO HOLD PRUNING KNIFE

RIGHT   WRONG

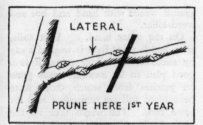

LATERAL

↓

PRUNE HERE 1ST YEAR

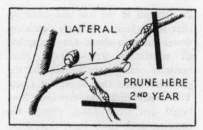

LATERAL

↓

PRUNE HERE 2ND YEAR

out overcrowding shoots, especially in the middle of the bush, so letting in air and light and making fruit picking easier next season. Cut back new growth at the end of the main branches to a bud pointing outwards about halfway down. But if the birds are unusually troublesome in your district

and peck at the buds, leave pruning until spring.

With redcurrants, shorten all side shoots (laterals) in winter to three or four buds, and cut back the growths at the ends of the main branches to an outside bud, leaving about six inches of new growth each year.

WINTER SPRAYING

Thorough spraying at the right times is probably the most important step you can take towards more and better fruit. Spraying in winter kills the eggs of Aphides (Greenfly), Apple Sucker, Red Spider, Capsid Bug and Winter Moths. Between the beginning of December and the end of January, you should spray your apples and pears once, either with a tar-oil spray ($\frac{1}{2}$ pint tar-oil to 1 gallon water) if Aphides or Apple Sucker are the troublesome pests, or with Dinitro-cresol petroleum oil (D.N.C. for short) if the other pests mentioned also need to be controlled. D.N.C. can be applied as late as the first half of March.

With plums and damsons, spray as for apples up to the middle of January. Don't delay until after the end of January or the crop may be seriously affected. Spraying time for goose-berries is up to the middle of January and for blackcurrants up to the end of that month.

So you will see that by choosing a date between early December and mid-January you could spray your apples, pears, plums, blackcurrants and gooseberries at one go.

Here are some important *spraying* points to bear in mind—

* Don't alter the proportions recommended for making up the sprays. Stronger mixtures may do more harm than good ; weaker sprays may not be effective.

* Mix and strain all sprays thoroughly before use. A piece of coarse muslin makes a good strainer.

* Spray thoroughly ; every part of the tree or bush must be drenched, especially the twigs.

* Don't spray in the rain, when rain is likely, or during frosty or windy weather.

* Cover any vegetable crops under

COVERED PLANTS

or near the trees, to prevent damage when using tar-oil or D.N.C. sprays; spring cabbages, for instance, are spoiled by the spray. Failing anything better, use newspapers.

* Take care not to damage flowering plants and hedges, especially your neighbour's, over the fence; if accidently sprayed, they should be thoroughly washed with clean water, using the garden hose before the spray has time to dry.

* Wash the spraying equipment after use.

* Don't make up more spray than you need for a day's work.

The quantity of spray needed will, of course, vary with the number and size of your trees and bushes. For fruit trees, here is a table showing the average quantities required according to the size of the tree—

Diameter of spread of tree	No. of gallons of dilute wash per tree
10-12 ft.	1
12-15 ft.	$1\frac{1}{2}$
15-18 ft.	$2\frac{1}{4}$
18-21 ft.	3
21-24 ft.	4

For blackcurrants, gooseberries and other bush fruit, 1 gallon of spray will be enough for up to 10 bushes, according to size.

Any form of syringe can be used for spraying, provided that you can reach every twig with it. Or you could use a stirrup and bucket pump of the A.R.P. variety, though you'll need two persons to work it. For really big trees, a barrow type of sprayer would be necessary.

WINTER MANURING

Because conditions vary from district to district, even from garden to garden —manuring advice must be fairly general, and these notes deal only with what can be done at this time of year. Fruit trees and bushes, like vegetables, need fertilisers—and in the right proportions; for instance, nitrogen is needed to make shoots and leaves, though too much of it will produce rank growth but little fruit. If your apples and pears are not so vigorous as they should be, they can be encouraged by dressing the ground around the trees in winter with hoof-and-horn at the rate of 3-4 oz. per square yard. Alternatively, sulphate of ammonia, applied in early spring at the rate of 1-2 oz. per sq. yd., will prove equally effective.

Apples and pears (not so much) need potash, especially on light soils. But that's difficult to come by and you may have to rely on wood ash from your bonfires. This should be kept in a dry place until you apply it to the ground in April. And don't forget that your gooseberries would like as much wood ash as you can give them; if there's any to spare the redcurrants and raspberries would appreciate it. Blackcurrants don't need it so much.

Every second winter give your plums a dressing of 2-3 ozs. of bone meal.

Don't forget at this time of year to fork lightly over the ground around fruit trees and bushes. But be careful about the raspberries: their roots are near the surface and they don't like being disturbed.

Issued by the
MINISTRY OF
AGRICULTURE AND
FISHERIES

Wt. T13004/8722 125M 7/4 CN&CoLtd.

HOW TO PRUNE
FRUIT TREES
AND BUSHES

**DIG FOR VICTORY
LEAFLET   NO.25**

*Small guides were also produced to give
advice on specific gardening tasks.*

December

Despite the promising heading of 'Vol. I No. 12', the December *Allotment & Garden Guide* was the last issue and Volume 2 was never released. For the previous six months the Guides had carried the warning 'Please Keep', suggesting that a decision had already been made not to embark on Volume 2. The final instalment looked backwards as well as forwards. Conditions had been difficult, and remained so, but with seed supplies nearing normal and National Growmore fertiliser still available, gardeners were all set to Dig for Plenty – the government's post-war slogan.

The return of peacetime did see an almost immediate return to the view that a woman's place was in the kitchen and not on the allotment. Having urged women to do their bit on the plot and celebrated as thousands of them did so, the Ministry of Agriculture now relegated them back to the kitchen, hopefully delighted to receive a Christmas gift of 'Domestic Preservation of Fruit and Vegetables'.

The Guide envisaged the '*thrifty housewife*' waiting at home for her '*good man*' to bring home the vegetables that she could not afford to buy in the shops. The 'good man' had not had an easy 1945. Pests had been especially numerous, the weather especially poor, and rain especially plentiful. The Garden Guide hoped that, despite these adversities, its readers would '*bind closer...to the most enduring hobby of all*'. The reality was that the next decade would see a rapid decline in numbers of allotment holders and vegetable gardeners. Prepared to Dig for Victory, they preferred not to dig just for the sake of it!

MINISTRY OF AGRICULTURE

ALLOTMENT &

Garden Guide

VOL. 1 No. 12   **DECEMBER - 1945**

> *"In a drear-nighted December*
> *Too happy, happy tree,*
> *Thy branches ne'er remember*
> *Their green felicity."*

Unlike Keats's "too happy tree," we gardeners are apt, in the words of another poet, to indulge in the pastime of "I remember." And no doubt on more than one drear December night we shall sit by the fire thinking of our successes and failures of the past season in the vegetable and fruit gardens. We shall no doubt do a bit of moralising, too—possibly make good resolutions about being more timely in our operations next year. And as it's the month traditionally associated with goodwill to all men, we may be thinking about Christmas presents, not only those we may perchance expect but those we will like to give. So as there's very little we may be able to do outdoors this time of year, save possibly getting on with digging any spare ground that's not frostbound, let us do a bit of fireside gardening, with a bit of looking back and perhaps a glance into the future.

Looking back

It has been said that of all dead things only the past smells sweet. How does the past "smell" to you as you look back on your gardening year? If you were successful, no doubt the past year was "sweet." (But were there no crops that failed you?). If, however, your season was very mixed, you will no doubt be thinking of the weather or the pests or both.

The weather is always with us to grouse about, and 1945 was on the whole a poor year. In the first place we got away to a bad start. The Januarys of 1940 and 1945 were among the coldest of the last half century, and those of us who put off doing things before Christmas were less inclined to do anything for a long time afterwards. The beginning of the year's offensive

 was far too long delayed on many allotments, with the result that the "diggers" were for ever trying to catch up on the jobs to be done and seldom succeeded, and the soil lacked the weathering influence that benefits land dug during winter.

Too much rain, not enough sun—that was 1945. Tomatoes loomed large in the minds of most of our gardeners. They were late in most places owing to the lack of ripening sun, and numerous were the enquiries for hints on speeding up ripening. Some people had trouble with their runners : the flowers would not set. In built-up areas there were no bees to do the job of pollination and some allotment holders were unable to give the flowers the fine misty spraying that could have helped. Or it may have been that watering, where possible, was irregular and the land dried out too quickly, which was a trouble on the Ministry's own demonstration allotments in Hyde Park. On some plots marrows suddenly died off and there was little that could be done about that.

No doubt owing to the American "invasion" of this country many gardeners became much interested in sweet corn, and there were complaints about delayed ripening. On the Ministry's own plots, however, which are by no means ideal, the variety

"John Innes Hybrid," which is early maturing, did well and aroused much interest. The various herbs grown there also came in for attention and later on there is a note on this subject.

But perhaps the subject that was most often raised by visitors to the Ministry's plots was pests and diseases. Greenfly and blackfly, of course, are nearly always with us and occasioned many enquiries, but the "Cabbage White" butterfly came in for the most vituperation. The Ministry's woman demonstrator reports that one Sunday morning in a Sussex cottage she picked about fifty caterpillars off the walls upstairs and downstairs, and that a cabbage field nearby was "skeletonised" in groups. We read that ninety-nine years ago passengers on a cross-Channel boat found the sun obscured for hundreds of yards by a cloud of this pest flying from France to England. This year their descendants must have come in even greater numbers, and only those gardeners who took prompt action by spraying and hand-picking managed to save their green crops, especially the Brussels, from being turned into skeletons.

INVASION OF BRITAIN—1945

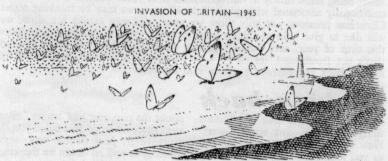

Does vegetable growing pay?

During the last year or so the question has often been raised "Does an allotment pay?" Following Dr. Joad's example, it all depends on what you mean by pay. And whom does it pay? The Ministry of Agriculture has from time to time published the financial returns of demonstration allotments in different parts of the country, which showed that crops to the value of anything from £20 to £30, at retail prices, had been grown on 10 rods. Records of about a hundred 10-rod plots kept in 1940-41 showed an average of nearly 20 lb. edible weight of vegetables weekly in winter, the figures for the other seasons being, spring, 11 lb.; summer, 12 lb.; autumn, 15 lb.

Of course, there is far more to it than mere financial returns, though the thrifty housewife would be the first to acknowledge what a help it is, in these days of high prices, to have her "good man" bring her home vegetables in variety that cost a good deal to buy in the shops. She knows, too, how important a part vegetables play in maintaining family health.

The "good man" himself may not, perhaps, have thought about the allotment first from the economic angle. His attitude depends on whether he had a plot before the war, or took it on after the war started. No doubt the pre-war allotment holder felt the call of the land and the allotment was his pastime. The war-time cultivator would probably say that he wanted to make sure of vegetables for his family; in some cases he may have feared a food shortage or patriotically desired to help the national food situation. Whatever the motive that prompted the man to take on an allotment, he has benefited himself: he is generally better in health because of the exercise, better in spirit because cultivating his plot took his mind off the war or the burdens of office or workshop; he has benefited his family by providing fresh vegetables that kept them fit—and, incidentally helped his wife in trying to make ends meet and avoid queues;

he and his fellow "Victory Diggers" benefited their country by contributing in every year of the war a substantial and indispensable quantity of food to the national larder, without which the nation might well have had to go short, not only of vegetables but of other food which our farmers have been enabled to grow through the "Victory Diggers'" efforts. Does an allotment pay? Emphatically it does, provided it is well managed and efficiently cultivated. And the same goes for the private vegetable garden, too.

SPRING
11 lbs. WEEKLY

SUMMER
12 lbs. WEEKLY

AUTUMN
15 lbs. WEEKLY

WINTER
20 lbs. WEEKLY

About those TOOLS

Now is the time of year when you ought to take stock of your tools and buy any replacements, so that you will be ready for next season. There are a number of little things that matter when you are choosing new tools and the following hints may be helpful, especially in these days when quality seems to have suffered. When getting a spade, make sure that it's comfortable to handle. And see that the wide ends of the grain are at the side of the handle, otherwise it might split later on and tear your hands, or even break with a heavy strain. The rivet on the shaft should be well sunk and smoothed off, or again your hands may suffer.

A good fork should be properly forged and should ring clearly when you knock the prongs on the floor. Gardeners generally prefer a flattish trowel, for the very round sort makes the work much harder. Take care, too, in buying rakes and hoes. A very thin handle is not comfortable to grip, so try it in the shop before you take it away. The hoe should be properly welded, as it will have some tough work to do when the ground is very hard. The teeth of an iron rake should be riveted firmly or they will soon fall out.

Better still, get one that is cast in one piece.

If you have no need to buy, it will repay you to take care of what you have. See that all your tools are stored in a safe place. Spades, hoes, trowels, rakes and forks should be thoroughly cleaned, dried and well oiled before being put away for their short rest. Nets should also be well dried and neatly rolled up, the garden line cleaned of soil and stored safely in a dry place, barrows put under cover and, if necessary, given a coat of paint—if you can get it. Well-kept garden tools make the work so much easier, for a sharp, well-kept spade demands far less energy than one that has not had its regular cleaning and oiling.

Christmas and the gardener

Gardeners are a clanny, generous crowd as a rule, and the coming of the first peace-time Christmas may afford them an opportunity to give presents that may come in useful next gardening season—possibly for many seasons to come, according to the kind of gift. Most of us gardeners are seldom blessed with too many tools, for instance. And there is a

wide range from a trowel costing a few shillings to a wheelbarrow for a few pounds.

Then a good gardening book is always a good "buy." To-day, more than ever before, gardeners are seeking knowledge and generally the bookseller has a section of his shelves devoted to gardening books from a few shillings upwards. Or if you

4

want to give something cheaper, your friend would value the Royal Horticultural Society's excellent book "The Vegetable Garden Displayed," which is lavishly illustrated with instructional photographs and can be obtained from the Society at Vincent Square, London, S.W.1., price 2/- post free. Or—cheaper still and, in effect, a practical Christmas "card"—is any one of the Ministry's own bulletins :—"Food from the Garden," 3d. (4d.), "Fruit from the Garden," 3d. (4d.), "Pests and Diseases in the Vegetable Garden," 4d. (5d.). Incidentally, a revised and up-to-date edition of the last-named has recently been published. If there's a lady in the case, she may like "Domestic Preservation of Fruit and Vegetables," 1s. 6d. (1s. 8d.) or the cheaper bulletin "Preserves from the Garden," 4d. (5d.). The figures in brackets are inclusive of postage. All these bulletins can be had from H.M. Stationery Office, York House, Kingsway, London W.C.2., or through any bookseller.

In more normal times another useful present would be a year's sub-scription to one of the gardening periodicals ; but in these days of continuing paper shortage these journals cannot print enough copies to meet the heavy demands made on them.

If you are a member of an allotment or horticultural society, why not make your friend a member by paying his or her first subscription ? For knowledge gained from these personal contacts is sometimes more helpful than the written word.

Gifts of plants, seeds or bulbs are always appreciated, so what about a collection of vegetable seeds, a few fruit trees or bushes, or perhaps some attractive flowering plants not needing too much attention in these days of scanty leisure. Or a bag of shallot sets, a pinch of a well-guarded strain of onion seed, a few divisions from a clump of chives or other useful perennials, all make timely and acceptable Christmas offerings. Hundreds of thousands have found out during the war the pleasures and excitements of growing plants and tending living things, so it will be in keeping with the spirit of Christmas to give them something that will enhance that satisfaction and bind them closer to the most enduring hobby of all.

Looking forward

When we are doing our fireside gardening round about Christmas we shall like to have our seedsman's catalogue to study. So if you have not already got it, send for it on receipt of this Guide. And remember that he has still got his labour difficulties and that he would appreciate it if you sent in your order early, not delay ordering until the last moment just before sowing time, when there is always a hectic rush at seedsmen's premises. Order your seed potatoes early, too, for transport is far from being normal.

The seed position looks like being pretty favourable, except that broad beans are likely to be short. But don't feel aggrieved if you still can't get all your favourite varieties. You'll know only too well that the end of the war has not meant the solution of all our problems.

As to artificial fertilizers—or "mineral" fertilizers, which is the better term—the situation can be summed up in two words—"no change." There is likely to be a sufficiency of "National Growmore," the balanced fertilizer sponsored by the Government, which has been tried by many gardeners and found quite satisfactory.

Make a new plan for the cropping of your allotment or garden, being guided by your past experience of what to grow and the quantity of each kind.

What about some HERBS?

When planning your garden or allotment for next year, bear herbs in mind. If you already have one or two kinds, try some of the less common, to give variety of flavour to your vegetables. Herbs are not difficult to grow, for many are perennial; once established, they go on growing year after year. Plants can be raised from seeds; but as this is rather a slow business, see if your friends can let you have some cuttings or pieces for next spring and early summer.

In the meantime get the soil ready by digging deeply and working in plenty of well-rotted manure or compost. Once the plants are

growing, only surface cultivation will be possible, so it is worth while making a good job of the digging. It will then only be necessary to keep weeds in check and the soil aerated by hoeing during the growing season. It is better to group herbs together in one bed. Mint prefers partial shade and not too dry a soil; but most of the others like a sunny, well-drained soil.

There are several forms of mint, but the nicest for mint sauce and other flavouring is spearmint. "Runners," or side branches of an old plant, root very easily and may be planted in March or April. If there is no natural shade, a mulch of rotted leaves will help to keep the roots cool.

Besides the ordinary thyme, the lemon-flavoured kind should be grown. Both prefer a warm soil. Cuttings can be taken during the early summer, or old plants can be lifted and divided into convenient pieces for replanting in Spring. It is a good plan to do this every two or three years, as old plants often get "leggy" and bare of young shoots.

Sage is another herb that can be propagated by cuttings, preferably with a "heel"—a piece of the old stem attached to the slip. In some districts they need the protection of a cold frame for rooting. April and May are the best months for this.

Pot marjoram or sweet marjoram, the best-known forms, can be raised from cuttings, though they are often treated as annuals, seeds being sown each April.

Chervil and savory are two more herbs that are often raised from seeds, though savory can also be propagated in the same way

MINT

MARJORAM

SAGE

CHERVIL

SAVORY

TARRAGON

as thyme. Chervil is used fresh, but savory can be dried like sage.

Chives are among the easiest herbs to grow and the "grass" or stems, either fresh or dried, can be used for flavouring instead of onions. The more it is cut, the better the plant grows. The plants make a delightful edging to the herb bed and new plantings can be made in autumn or spring by lifting and dividing old plants into single bulbs or groups of two or three.

Parsley, too, is suitable as an edging plant. To get successional supplies it is best to sow three times : February or March, April, or early May, and again in July. The last sowing will give fresh parsley until severe frosts cut down the plants.

Fresh sprigs of parsley are generally used, but it is not always known that the shoots can be dried for winter use. To keep the colour as much as possible, the drying must be done quickly, and it is best to put the bunches in a cool oven.

Among the less common herbs are tarragon, wormwood, southern-wood, basil, balm and fennel. Now is the time to look round and see where you can get seeds, cuttings or pieces to make a start next spring.

First aid for the birds

In winter, when so many of our useful insect-eating birds are away overseas, we can do much to help our feathered friends that are still with us. Prominent among them are the robin, the wren, the hedge-sparrow, the song-thrush, and the various species of tits.

There are two ways in which we can help them ; we can provide food tables—a very pleasant help in time of trouble : we can provide nest-boxes—as part of a "long-term" policy.

To deal first with food, let us be clear that in open weather, even in winter, all these birds can take care of themselves without our help ; but given a prolonged spell of frost and snow like we had last February, with the ground iron-hard for days on end and natural food almost unobtainable, then a little timely aid from us may make all the difference between life and death for the birds.

Now we all know that human food must not be wasted : in fact it's illegal. But there are some things we may still offer the birds without breaking the law. Here are a few suggestions for their food table :— bacon rind, either hung up in strips for the tits or minced for all comers, crumbs swept from the breakfast table, fish skin and bones, cheese rind, and bits of fat from the dog's meat man. And don't forget that in really hard weather unfrozen drinking water is as important to the birds as food.

Now as to nest-boxes. If you do it now, there is still time to make and put up a nest-box in your garden. With luck, a pair of great or blue tits may rear a brood in it, to their great advantage and yours. Members of the tit family do not begin to nest until the end of March or the beginning of April, but the longer you

give them to get used to the box the better. Tits have a habit of looking over possible nesting sites very early in the year. There are, of course, other kinds of birds that will take over nest-boxes properly made and placed.

Size, shape and position of a nest-box are all very important. How to make it would take up too much space in this Guide, but, if you are really interested, write to the Ministry at Berri Court Hotel, St. Annes, Lytham St. Annes, Lancs., for Advisory Leaflet No. 212.

Wt T14780/8752 125M 7/4 CN&CoLtd

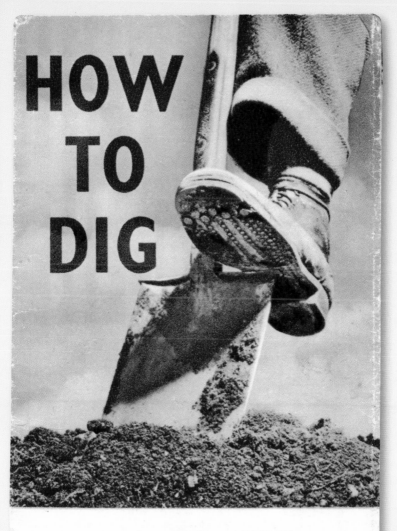

HOW TO DIG

DIG FOR VICTORY LEAFLET
NUMBER 20   (NEW SERIES)

ISSUED BY THE MINISTRY OF AGRICULTURE

Perhaps the most well-known image of the Dig for Victory campaign adorns the cover of a leaflet that explains to the novice gardener 'How to Dig'.

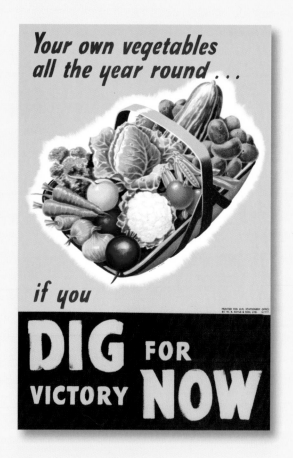

Acknowledgements

Many thanks to Mike Brown for images from his collection.
Many thanks to Jon Mills for images from his collection.